Balancing Your Career, Family and Life

The Lifeplanner Series

There are many situations in life for which your education, your parents or your experience simply have not prepared you. In this major new series, Kogan Page and *The Daily Telegraph* have joined forces with a team of expert writers to provide practical, down-to-earth information and advice for anyone encountering such a situation for the first time.

The series addresses personal finance and consumer issues in a jargon-free, readable way, taking the fear out of planning your life. So whether you are thinking about buying a house, having a baby or just deciding what to spend your first pay cheque on, the Lifeplanner series will help you do so wisely.

Titles available are:

The Young Professional's Guide to Personal Finance
Your First Home: A Practical Guide to Buying and Renting
Making the Most of Being a Student

Forthcoming titles are:

Your First Investment Portfolio
Your Child's Education

Available from all good booksellers. For further information on the series, please contact:

Kogan Page
120 Pentonville Road
London
N1 9JN
Tel: 0171 278 0433
Fax: 0171 837 6348
e-mail: kpinfo@kogan-page.co.uk

Balancing Your Career, Family and Life

CARY L. COOPER and SUZAN LEWIS

**KOGAN
PAGE**

YOURS TO HAVE AND TO HOLD
BUT NOT TO COPY

First published in 1998

Kogan Page Limited
120 Pentonville Road
London N1 9JN

© Cary L. Cooper and Suzan Lewis, 1998

British Library Cataloguing in Publication Data

A CIP record for this book is available from the British Library.

ISBN 0 7494 2528 8

Typeset by JS Typesetting, Wellingborough, Northants.
Printed and bound in Great Britain by Clays Ltd, St Ives Plc

Contents

1 Introduction

More and more women and men are balancing careers and family nowadays. This book explores some of the major issues faced by dual-career partners, who are a growing proportion of the workforce. Based on more than a decade of research with dual-earner couples and their managers, we discuss the strategies that they adopt and we also consider steps that employers can take to find possible solutions to dilemmas which threaten to hold back the careers and reduce the potential organizational contribution of some of the most talented and highly trained members of the workforce.

The Changing Workforce

The once traditional family pattern of breadwinner father, homemaker mother and children is now a minority form in much of the industrialized world.[1] The majority of two-parent households with children have both parents in employment. A growing number of working women and men of all ages also have caring responsibilities for elderly or disabled relatives.[2] With the increasing numbers of dual-earner and single-parent families, high rates of divorce, medical advances and the growing elderly population, most adult family members combine employment with family caring at some stage in their life cycle.

Both women's and men's family roles are changing dramatically, although the trends are more marked in women, with men continuing to endorse more traditional views than women on gender roles and particularly domestic work.[3] Although still more attached to family than men, women are increasingly valuing a career and financial independence over a solely domestic role.[4] However, this has not led to a wholehearted acceptance of the traditional male work ethic, with its emphasis on total dedication of time to the workplace. Indeed, there is evidence that more men, as well as women, are valuing shorter working hours and would trade income for shorter hours, enabling them to spend time with their family and achieve a more balanced life.[5] One suggestion is that this may be a reaction to the excessive competitiveness of the 1980s.[6]

This trend has numerous potential advantages. A balanced life can provide multiple sources of satisfaction,[7] contribute towards quality of life and well-being of men and women and of those for whom they care,[8] and enable people to make an optimum contribution at work.[9] Currently, however, combining family and employment roles often creates stress, overload and conflict.[10]

It is important to look for ways in which dual-earner partners can manage their work and family lives to gain the most satisfaction and minimize stress. Some people feel that managing work and family is just an individual problem. But this is not true. Dual-earner family stress affects individuals, families, workplaces and society. This means that work and family management is an organizational issue as well as an issue for dual-earner couples themselves. There are a number of reasons why workplaces have to change to accommodate the needs of such families.

Why the Workplace Has to Change

The potential for stress for dual-earner partners working in traditional organizations is just one of many reasons why organizations must change and why the traditional male work ethic must be challenged to accommodate the new workforce:

Stress

Our research shows that dual-earner men and women who work in unresponsive, inflexible organizations are more dissatisfied with their jobs and suffer higher levels of stress than those in organizations which respond to their needs for a healthy balance between work and family.[11] They are often overloaded by the demands of work and family, or suffer conflict between the demands of each, especially if they have young children or elderly or sick relatives. This can cause poor motivation and productivity, ill-health and high staff turnover. A study of highly successful and healthy executives of both sexes in the US demonstrated that these people are not workaholics, catching only occasional glimpses of their families. Rather they are people who have achieved a healthy balance in their lives, with a satisfying level of involvement in both family and work.[12] There is mounting evidence that supportive workplace policies and practices enhance employees' feelings of control and reduce uncertainty, anxiety and stress.[13] So responding to the need of dual-earner women and men is important for the health of the workforce. This involves questioning some basic and often taken for granted assumptions about gender, careers and the nature of work.

Demographic Changes

Demographic changes (a falling birth rate, an ageing population) mean that organizations can no longer rely on the traditional recruitment pool of young white males. There is a risk of skills shortages in many crucial areas of work. Of course women have always been recruited into the work-force, but many are still employed in low-paid jobs with few opportunities for advancement, often under-utilizing their abilities in order to find part-time or flexible work to fit in with their family responsibilities. Organizations which continue to utilize women chiefly as cheap labour or in undemanding jobs, fail to recruit and promote from the widest pool of talent. Retention of trained staff will also become a problem in organizations which do not allow sufficient flexibility for men and women with family responsibilities. Companies adopting a long-term view recognize the need to develop all their employees and to ensure a sufficient number of skilled people as a key advantage if they are to prosper in the global economy.

Britain in Europe

In terms of public policy to facilitate harmony between work and family, Britain has lagged behind the rest of Europe. In most other European states public provision of childcare facilities is much greater than that available in the UK. (It could hardly be less.) Recently, maternity leave provisions have been enhanced to conform to European Health and Safety law so that all women are now entitled to some leave. However the opt out from the Maastricht Social Chapter, negotiated by the former Conservative government, means that Britain is the only European state not required to provide parental leave for fathers as well as mothers, nor family leave to deal with caring emergencies. The provision of parental leave has the potential to benefit not only employees and their families, but also employing organizations. Our research shows very clearly that lack of opportunities for fathers to be involved with children from an early age, and particularly lack of entitlement to leave for family emergencies, create considerable strain. This, in turn, impinges on employees' ability to do their jobs. The lack of policies such as these communicates a failure to value employees with family commitments which engenders low morale and often leads experienced workers to leave for a more flexible job, or to move into self employment to obtain the flexibility needed. Until now, lack of government intervention has placed more responsibility on employers to provide the facilities which are mandated by governments elsewhere. Organizations which implemented family leave policies may have gained a competitive edge in terms of recruitment and retention. It will, of course, still be possible to retain this competitive edge in the context of mandatory leave, by providing more than the statutory minimum of benefits, for example by providing paid leave.

Equal Opportunities

Most organizations now have an equal opportunities policy and many also have equal opportunities officers to ensure optimum policies and practices. For 'equality of opportunity' to be a reality, however, it is important to go beyond making provisions for women, such as part-time work or career breaks, while at the same time expecting men who are committed to their careers to work full-time and continuously. Provisions to facilitate the balancing of work and family, apart from maternity leave, are always available to men, by law, but the perceived cost to men of using these provisions is usually formidable. What is needed is a more fundamental culture change. It will be important to question basic organizational and managerial values, such as the myth that long hours are necessary to demonstrate commitment, and to work out ways of enabling both men and women to make an optimum contribution to the organization as well as within the family.

Valuing Diversity Makes Good Business Sense

Initially equal opportunity arguments tended to focus on ethical and social values, and the need to avoid litigation, rather than the many commercial benefits of a balanced workforce. More recently there has been a greater focus on managing diversity which develops and complements traditional approaches to equal opportunities, with a greater recognition of business advantages. According to the Institute of Personnel and Development, managing diversity is based on the concept that people should be valued as individuals for reasons related to business interest as well as for moral and social reasons.[14] The managing diversity argument goes beyond gender, race and disability to recognize that people from diverse backgrounds can bring fresh ideas and perceptions which can improve efficiency, productivity and quality of services. Managing diversity can thus help organizations to nurture creativity and tap hidden potential for growth and improved competitiveness.

The business-led campaign, Opportunity 2000, which encourages companies to work towards more equal representation of men and women at all levels, makes a strong business case for managing diversity. The campaign points to companies such as Digital and Xerox, where equal opportunities or diversity initiatives have resulted in improved communication, effective team work, increased productivity and, ultimately, higher profits.[15] Research in the US also demonstrates the competitive advantages to be reaped at all levels of an organization from restructuring workplace systems to recognize employees' work and family needs.[16]

The benefits of removing obstacles to career success of diverse employees include:

▌ *Development of all the workforce.* Companies which enable employees to combine career and family life, and remove artificial barriers to promotion will secure a good return on human resources investment. High calibre employees will choose to work for, and be committed to, these organizations.

▌ *Getting close to clients or customers.* Management needs to be sensitive to the major issues affecting their customers. A balanced workforce, with men and women (and representatives of different ethnic and other groups) at all levels is better able to respond to customer or client needs.

▌ *The value of differences.* Heterogeneous teams are more creative and innovative than homogeneous ones. The management of diverse groups also requires specific skills. The enhanced development of managers, which results from managing diversity, enables them to be more flexible and to be better able to respond to change.

In the remainder of this book we explore issues facing dual-earner families and the organizations in which they are employed, and suggest practical steps that can be taken by dual-earner partners themselves, as well by employers who wish to recruit, retain and motivate people who are highly committed to their work, and who also have a healthy commitment to and involvement in life beyond work.

2 Stress and Coping at Work

Although careers provide a major source of life satisfaction, work can also be a source of stress. Occupational stress may show itself in a range of symptoms including physical illness, psychological distress and low productivity. The causes of stress at work are usually described primarily in terms of job demands, but the demands of the home, and particularly the problem of juggling family and work, are also significantly related to occupational stress, particularly for dual-earner families. A demanding career may involve long hours of work, which combined with the demands of domestic life and childcare can cause you to feel overloaded, unless there is adequate support. There may also be conflict between the demands of career and family roles, especially when work schedules are incompatible with family life.

In order to examine sources and consequences of stress, we surveyed 310 dual-earner spouses, in a range of occupations. Most of the respondents reported some feelings of overload and conflict, although the majority were coping well and avoiding major symptoms of stress. Although the dual-career lifestyle is very demanding, it is not necessarily stressful. Indeed, multiple demands can be very satisfying if they are well managed.

> I have the satisfaction of knowing I have reached the heights of my career and not missed out on family life and motherhood. (company executive, female)

Nevertheless, some dual-career spouses in our study did report symptoms of stress, and most felt that the demands made upon them could be reduced. Most of the pressures they reported were the consequence, either directly or indirectly, of traditional gender stereotypes and expectations, and of assumptions about the way work should be organized. In the past, men could spend long hours in work while their 'homemaker' wives sacrificed their own careers, and this has created a norm to which contemporary men and women are expected to conform. This can present problems for egalitarian dual-earner families, particularly those with children.

Need for a 'Wife' at Home

Although women are increasingly represented in all areas of work, men continue to dominate the higher echelons of professional and managerial worlds. Most have achieved success with the support of a partner who is either a full-time housewife or who has continued to fulfil major domestic tasks in addition to paid work. This pattern continues even among some of today's dual-career couples:

> Michael works long hours. He'd rather work doing what he's qualified to do and pay someone else to do menial tasks. He's happy to take the baby for a walk but he won't cook a meal. I spend more time with the children, and do the work at weekends as we have no living-in help. I accept that his career has priority. (personnel officer, female)

This level of support enables an ambitious man or less frequently, an ambitious woman, to maintain a single-minded level of work involvement, to work long hours, to travel away from home and to relocate when necessary. During the stage when careers are being developed, the workaholic lifestyle may leave little time for life outside work, and even in single breadwinner families this can cause considerable family strain. A woman who caters for every-day needs enables a man to work at a relentless pace and perform at his peak. Women must compete on these terms. Frequently they lament that they too 'need a wife', partic-ularly if they are working in competitive male-dominated occupations. A female sales manager explained:

> I'm in what is basically a male-oriented world. It is unusual for a woman to be in the sales field and I can see why. Most of my colleagues have got wives or girlfriends to go home to. They fulfil this other function of fitting in the daily chores which need to be done in order to be up and starting at base point again the next day. For us it's different, we tend to be running to catch up with ourselves before we've got up, so to speak. I think that's true of most people who have jobs where the expectation is that someone else is available to take on the pressure of organizing one's life.

Many occupations are so demanding that they can be considered a 'two-person career', which implies that the back-up support of a partner is essential. Partners, usually women, may provide services such as editing or clerical assistance directly substituting for the work of a paid employee, and assist with entertaining and socializing which can enhance a partner's position in the organization. These services are on top of providing emotional and domestic support. Many companies recognize that a female partner is an asset, though they often fail to recognize that she may have her own career. The male partner of the career woman is often perceived as a liability:

> The company believes that men should have wives and that they are an advantage. If you move around a lot the wife can be looking after the children and buying a new house while he is at work. I don't have a wife to do that for me which makes life a bit difficult. (trainee manager, female)

When I go for interviews it is assumed that my having a wife
is a sign of maturity and stability, whereas I think a woman
with a husband and family is thought to show signs of being
tied down and inflexible. (engineer, male)

With the demise of the male breadwinner family, men as well
as women find the traditional male work orientation difficult
to accommodate with family life. There may be company
pressure on men to conform to stereotypical roles and to
ensure that family commitments do not encroach upon work.
Often, however, the pressures are self-imposed, due to the
internalization of the macho work ethic and the need to
conform and compete on an equal basis with single-earners.

Competing in a male-dominated world, thus, means that
dual-earner women and men must often conform to the
example set by men pursuing 'two-person careers' with the
practical support of a partner.

In the remainder of this chapter, we consider some of the
work-related sources of stress experienced by dual-earner
partners as a consequence of the traditional model of work,
and examine some of the strategies used to cope with these
pressures.

Work Overload – Long Hours of Work and the Workaholic Syndrome

When you feel that your workload is so great that you are
constantly under pressure, you can be said to be suffering
from work overload. A civil servant and mother of a young
baby illustrates this problem:

I feel I've constantly got more things to do than I have time
for. It's partly because I work for a head of department who
is very good but very ambitious and pushes everyone else.
It's hard work keeping up with her. I just feel under constant
pressure the whole time.

For members of dual-earner partnerships, overload is usually a consequence of intense demands both at work and at home. Here we examine occupational demands in terms of hours at work and the potential for overload in the work situation. But work overload cannot be considered in isolation from family demands; the two spheres are inter-dependent.

In our survey, work overload emerged as a very significant source of stress for dual-earner couples, whether or not they had children. The habit of putting in long hours at work tends to be established early in a person's career, and is often perceived initially as an investment for the future. Indeed, long hours at the workplace, perhaps combined with additional studying, may be regarded as a necessary early foundation for career success.

> My hours according to the time clock in the office work out at about 48 to 50 hours a week and then I do another 18 hours at home because I am studying for an extra degree. Ann probably works from about 8.30 to 9.00ish in the morning until about 5.00 or 6.00 and then three nights a week on average when she has calls to make in the evenings and will arrive home anytime between 8.00 and 10.00. Both of us are at the stage in our careers when you have to put these hours in to climb up the ladder. The hours will diminish hopefully after four or five years. (lawyer, male, no children)

Once the pattern of devoting long hours to work has been established, it often becomes a permanent way of life. In many cases, this is because the work and the associated pressure and successes are experienced as rewarding and satisfying. You can become addicted to this way of life. This is the beginning of the _workaholic syndrome_. A lawyer who had decided with his partner that they would not have children explained:

I really enjoy the work I do so it doesn't matter if it spills over to the weekend. Maybe I'll get sick of it after ten or 20 years. But I think it's true to say that I enjoy stress anyway so I enjoy the long hours. I'm quite masochistic, I suppose. I know many of my colleagues see it more in terms of something you have to go through. It's a penance for the next few years. But I thrive on it.

Other people agree that working at a relentless pace becomes a way of life, but are less enthusiastic about it. A chartered accountant explained why she believed that substantial overtime becomes the norm in certain occupations:

I think that once people have qualified, perhaps doing all that studying gets them into the frame of mind of working long hours. They get used to it and also it cuts them off from a lot of interests and a lot of friends they had before. They used to study on top of a full day's work and then they tend to fill up this time with overtime and that becomes accepted as the norm. I don't think it's just in accountancy. I've seen it with friends in other professions too.

Long hours of work which replace time spent in studying or which are seen as an investment for the future by ambitious young people, create an expectation that people will be able to sustain patterns of work which later may be difficult to reconcile with family life. The problem is that when you *do* need to modify hours of work for family reasons it may then be seen by management as lack of commitment and ambition, and may be regarded by colleagues as professional suicide. A male sales manager maintained:

I have published office hours of 8.45 to 5.15, but nobody in my position can just work those kind of hours and survive in a competitive world.

Excess time given to work is time unavailable for family activities, for childcare, for domestic work and for family leisure activities. In single-earner couples, excessive work hours by the breadwinner often means that the woman has to raise the children virtually as a 'single parent'. For dual earners, long hours of work by both partners may leave little time for their relationship, while long hours spent at work by one partner usually increases the domestic duties of the partner, which can cause resentment. Several dual-career couples referred to problems created by their own and their partner's long hours of work, in terms of relationship or family disruption:

> I left my last job because of the hours really. I had to work late most evenings. When I got home the children were asleep, and I just never had any time with my husband except late in the evening when I was exhausted. I think the relationship would have broken up if I had continued. (catering manager, female)

British men, and also women who work full-time, work the longest hours in Europe. The long hours culture is based on the assumption that the longer people spend at the workplace, the more committed and productive they are.[1] In fact, long hours can be a sign of inefficiency. So, this not only makes it difficult to balance work and family, but is also counterproductive for the organization.

Schedule Incompatibility and Inflexibility

It is not only the number of hours worked which is potentially stressful for dual-earner couples, but also the extent to which each partner's schedule fits in with that of their partner and with other family needs. This incompatibility can be a source of considerable conflict, particularly for those with young families or other dependants. Rigid schedules of work can also create difficulties in dealing with unforeseen circumstances, such as hospital appointments. As well as work–family conflict, rigid work schedules are also associated with reduced job and life satisfaction and poor mental health.[2] Long or inconvenient hours of work are much less stressful if there is a degree of flexibility and control.[3] Flexibility allows partners, especially parents, to put in the necessary amount of time at work and to do so during hours that fit in with other demands, enabling you to collect children from school or to take time off when necessary and make up the hours when it is convenient.

In order to assess the extent of work–family management problems, we asked dual-earner partners (with and without children) to indicate how easy or difficult it was to adapt their work schedules for family reasons. We also asked how satisfied they were with the flexibility of their job. The responses varied to some extent with different occupations, but not surprisingly it was clear that parents of young children experienced many more problems than childless couples in fitting in work and family demands. However, the vast majority of both parents and non-parents, while accepting that certain aspects of their jobs, by their very nature, were not flexible, believed that it would be possible and desirable to have a greater level of flexibility and control over some aspects of their work schedules.

Conflict between the demands of professional and parental schedules occurs for both sexes, although it is usually greater for women.[4] However, those questioned felt that employers are often more tolerant of work–family conflicts in women than in men. A man who takes time off work to care for a sick child or who restricts his hours at work to accommodate childcare is often viewed as a less committed employee than one who does not allow family life to impinge upon work.[5] Also it is often assumed that family participation (by men and by women) is associated with decreased commitment and performance at work, but this ignores the fact that many people are highly committed to both domains. Inability to attend to family needs because of inflexible schedules can have a negative impact on productivity and efficiency and can be counterproductive, as this woman lecturer in a college of further education commented:

> OK so I'm there, I do not take time off because my child's ill. My contribution under stress having to be physically there and worried about her may be less valuable than if I had taken the time off and worked from home and made up the time later.

Spillover

Another source of pressure for dual-career couples is spillover from work to family. Spillover occurs in three different forms:

1 spillover of work itself into family time;

2 spillover of work attitudes into family interactions;

and

3 spillover of job satisfaction or stress to life outside work.

Spillover of Work into Family Time

Commitments beyond normal working hours include the need to bring work home, to attend meetings and conferences, to travel extensively, or even to go out in the evenings with colleagues. Such commitments can be enjoyable and are usually considered important from a career perspective, but if they occur frequently they can interfere with family life, causing conflict of loyalties. The wife of an executive who travelled regularly complained:

> It is very difficult when he works weekends. Being away a couple of nights in the week doesn't bother anybody. It's part of the job and we expect it. It's just fortunate I don't have to travel with my job, so that I'm here for the children. But it does affect our family life when he is away at weekends. That's when we could all be together as a family and relax a bit together.

Although overtime or bringing work home may impinge upon family time, it need not be stressful for the individual. If you can choose to work overtime when it is convenient you are in control and, therefore, experience less work–family conflict than those who have no choice. So control over working hours is an important 'feelgood' factor.

Spillover of Behaviour and Attitudes from Work to Family

In traditional families where work and family roles are segregated on the basis of gender, behaviours appropriate to each domain can be cultivated. Combining work and family roles in dual-career couples means that appropriate behaviours must be displayed in each domain by both partners; for example, assertive behaviour at work and nurturing behaviour at home. The tendency to combine certain stereotypical masculine and feminine traits, so as to react appropriately in a range of situations, is known as *androgyny*. Androgynous individuals tend to enjoy better mental health than stereotypical masculine or feminine individuals who are unable to adopt a dominant or caring attitude in the appropriate context.

Many occupations, particularly those which have traditionally been male-dominated, require individuals of both sexes to be competitive, assertive and achievement oriented – although the value of more feminine characteristics in the workplace and especially in management styles is increasingly acknowledged. Dual-earner partners who combine professional and family work, nevertheless, have to switch from the style of behaviour deemed appropriate at work to non-competitive behaviours at home. Inevitably, there are occasions when the switch cannot easily be made; when work attitudes and behaviours spill over to family interactions. A college lecturer complained of her sales manager husband:

> If I tell him about some success I've had at work, he immediately responds with something good he's done. I know he's used to competing all the time at work so that it just becomes a habit to try to outdo everybody else. But it's not what I want. I want him to share my successes, to praise me occasionally, not to feel that we are in competition.

It seems likely that the husband of this woman is displaying what is known as _Type A behaviour_. Type A individuals are competitive, hostile, extremely involved in their work, impatient and very time-urgent. Unlike more laid-back Type B individuals, Type A's try to achieve more and more in less and less time, and compete relentlessly with themselves and others. Type A individuals create a great deal of stress for themselves and may be vulnerable to stress-related illnesses, such as coronary heart disease. As Type A behaviour tends to be brought on by a specific situation, usually a competitive work context, it may be possible to be Type A at work yet be more relaxed at home. Nevertheless, one study of male administrators[6] found that the partners of Type A men reported much lower marital satisfaction than the partners of Type B men, which suggests that this behaviour does spill over into family life with unfortunate consequences. Many organizations encourage the Type A behaviour pattern, by an emphasis on competitiveness, tight deadlines and intense work involvement, but it is important to recognize that Type A behaviour can create family disharmony as well as increasing vulnerability to life-threatening, stress-related illness.

Spillover of Stress and Satisfaction

Does satisfaction or stress from work does spill over into family life and vice versa? It is possible that the two areas *compensate* for each other. The notion of compensation implies that satisfaction at work compensates for dissatisfaction at home and vice versa. Thus, an individual with a difficult relationship may put more effort into gaining satisfaction at work, and someone who is stressed at work will try harder to gain their satisfactions from their home life. While the idea of compensation seems plausible, the majority of research supports the notion of spillover.[7] Stress or satisfaction at work can have an impact on life outside work and relationships at home can affect experiences at work. Spillover can occur in either direction and may be positive or negative.

We found several examples of stress at work spilling over into family life. Stressed individuals are often aware of taking out their frustrations on their family, but are unable to prevent themselves from doing so:

When I have a particularly bad day at work I know I'm horrible to live with. I shout at the kids and take it out on my husband. I'm tense and bad tempered and it affects everyone, although I still manage to be nice to everyone at work. (personnel officer, female)

How Do People Cope?

During a series of interviews with dual-earner partners we asked them how they coped with the pressures of their lifestyle. A number of coping strategies emerged.

Questioning the Need for Long Hours and the Workaholic Syndrome

Several of the participants in our study questioned whether long hours and workaholism are really productive:

> The workaholic syndrome flourishes here. It is assumed that everybody who wants to get on will be prepared to put the organization first at all times. It's no good for marriages and I'm not convinced that it's really good for productivity and efficiency in the long term. (journalist, male)

> Most of the people I work with don't seem to value their time off. There's an awful lot of people who don't take their full holiday allocation and who work an awful lot of overtime. They seem almost obsessed with work and that's difficult because that becomes accepted as the norm. Really this often goes beyond the point of reason because they work overtime to the point where they must become fairly inefficient. When you are working until 1.00 in the morning and then coming back on the job at 7.00 in the morning, well, to me the work I would have done between 10.00p.m. and 7.00a.m., I could have done in half the time the next morning. (chartered accountant, female)

In fact there is evidence to support this view. People working shorter hours are often more organized, while long hours can be associated with accidents and mistakes.[8]

Choosing Part-time Work

Reducing the number of hours worked to part-time, especially during the years of early childrearing, can be one solution to work and family overload, but many people find this unacceptable because of the associated loss of benefits:

> You lose out on course development and promotion if you are part-time. You are not taken seriously. I'd like to have a part-time job in terms of having more time but it would be a disaster career-wise. I want to be taken seriously, not left out when decisions are taken, which is what happens to part-time staff. I've witnessed the decline of colleagues who have changed to part-time. (midwife tutor, female)

> I am committed to my profession and I want to be taken seriously but I don't want to be working all hours. I want some time with my children. I wish it were possible to work part-time without losing my foot on the ladder. (lecturer, father of two)

Part-time work does not have to be career limiting, however, as discussed in Chapter 6.

Coping with Heavy Workloads – Managing Time

A heavy workload can be less stressful if you use effective techniques of time management. Most of the couples we interviewed had found ways of managing their time, which enabled them, with varying degrees of success, to reduce their workload or to cope with short-term overload. Strategies used included:

Being assertive. Be clear about your goals and priorities. Be able to say 'no' to demands which may cause overload (see Chapter 7 for a fuller discussion of assertiveness). A lecturer who felt that she had, after much soul searching, reached a point at which she could now say 'no' explained:

> I'm managing my time a lot better now. I'm saying 'no' to people and I'm not giving them things when they want them if I can't manage it. I'm much clearer now about responsibilities and recognizing that I have some personal home responsibilities as well as work responsibilities.

Similarly, a chartered accountant explained how she had made life easier by stating explicitly what she was and was not willing to do in terms of overtime:

> To a certain extent I know I'm putting myself on the line, but I have stated that I'm only prepared to do a reasonable amount of overtime. When I think it is unreasonable I'll say I'm not doing it.

This fear of 'putting yourself on the line', however, may prevent many overburdened employees from taking such actions.

Establishing priorities and dealing with temporary situations. Often periods of excessive workload are inevitable and it is necessary to find ways of coping with these for a short duration. A chartered accountant described the problems of studying for exams in addition to full-time work while her daughter was a baby. In the face of enormous demands and potential conflicts, she and her husband organized their time in a way they found effective and satisfying:

> The way we worked it was that I worked during the week and did all my studying during the week too so we could have the weekends free. I think most students work two or possibly three evenings, have a couple of evenings off and plan to work on Sunday. I never did that. It was the

weekends when I had time for the baby. Dave did all the cooking and put Amy to bed in the week but I had the whole weekend free with her.

By being clear about this time plan, she was able to work without any feelings of guilt during the week, knowing that her weekends would be totally free. Equally, she did not feel guilty about not studying at weekends because of the clear allocation of time.

Although the period of raising young children may be of a longer duration than the period of study for professional examinations, it can also be regarded as a temporary situation in the perspective of a lifetime career.

Managing time as a couple. Some couples approached time management as a couple rather than as two separate individuals, recognizing their interdependence by developing joint strategies.

We tried to reconcile work and home by agreeing a timetable whereby I try to work early in the mornings. Mark does the breakfasts and I go to work at 7.30a.m. and then I'm home in time for when the nanny leaves in the evening and he can stay late if he needs to.

This appears to be a well thought out, workable and equitable solution. Interestingly, however, this woman felt that she had not completely escaped the impact of gendered expectations.

It's a way of coping and it works. But I was aware in suggesting it that I got the raw deal, because the kids are tired and grumpy in the evenings and putting them to bed is a struggle, while getting them up isn't. So I still think there's something about, as a woman, taking on the difficult bits, the nastiest bits.

Attempting to manage time as a couple frequently raises issues about responsibility, gender and 'the woman's lot'. Adjustments made to working hours to help balance the demands of two jobs and families tend to be more often made by the woman, while adjustments made by men are more likely to involve a reduction in time allocated to the family.[9] Nevertheless, there is a growing minority of couples for whom time management strategies favour the woman's career. This usually occurs when the woman's occupation involves less flexible hours than that of her partner, but it also requires an acceptance of non-traditional roles. The director of a small firm described his approach to the management of time, which was clearly organized around his wife's career and the demands of childcare:

> It's just a question of making the best use of time. I can't do anything before 10.00a.m. or after 4.00p.m. That doesn't bother me because it enables Margaret to hold down a secure and satisfying job and I make enough money to live on comfortably. I've got my work organized optimally during the hours available.

Coping with Spillover

The strategies used by our interviewees for coping with spillover ranged from creating clear boundaries between work and home, to taking more drastic steps, such as making a career change. It has been suggested that men tend to experience dual roles sequentially, while women experience them simultaneously.[10] This suggests that women will have more difficulty than men in creating clear boundaries between work and home, because they think about family much of the time. Preventing family from impinging on work is therefore more difficult for many women. Some people make a very conscious effort to compartmentalize their lives, so as to ensure that work attitudes and stress do not impinge on their life outside work.

> Once I close the office door that is it. I switch off completely and start to think about the children, the evening meal and so forth. I would never take work home. (solicitor, female)

In drawing boundaries, women in particular often experience conflict about areas related to professional development. Society tolerates ambitions in women but expects a less professional commitment in mothers. This means that some women have to assert the right to continue to build their careers after they have children. One way in which our respondents resolved conflict about additional commitments such as attending conferences, was to involve other family members. Others took care to explain and negotiate with other family members. It is easier to explain commitments to a partner than to children, but even quite young children can understand a situation which is clearly communicated to them. This can reduce guilt, particularly for mothers whose work spills into family time.

One mother who sometimes finds it necessary to work at home in the evenings and during weekends, and who has two young daughters said:

> It works because Mike is able to support me and play with them and he makes it understandable to them. We worked together to make it all right for them. I don't feel guilty.

It is much more difficult to cope with work stress and dissatisfaction which spill over to create tension at home. Setting boundaries works in some cases, but it is difficult to switch off feelings of anxiety, depression or dissatisfaction which are symptoms of stress at work. Sometimes it is necessary to take action to provide the space and time to get things into perspective. One respondent described how a period of study, away from her job, enabled her to recognize the stress she had been suffering, which in her case led to a decision to make a career change.

> Intellectually I can do all the job analysis and stress analysis stuff and recognize it in that sense. But it was only being away from this environment that I actually experienced the change. Being a student I had no responsibility, no pressure. I could manage without working evenings and weekends. Above all, the practical elements of the course gave me the chance to do something I enjoyed and could do well. I suppose what it did was to give me some confidence back, in that there was no recognition for competence in my job. I suddenly found that I could enjoy life. I certainly became an easier person to live with. I was no longer grumpy and bad tempered with Ben and the girls all the time. I enjoy my work and I'm a nicer person at home.

It is necessary to recognize work stress and the effect of spillover on family life, before steps can be taken to change the situation. A period of 'time out' can be instrumental in enabling individuals to recognize the stress they are experiencing, and to see how their life both at home and at work might be different.

How Can Organizations Help?

Organizations can adapt in a number of ways:

▌ The traditional male breadwinner/homemaker wife set up creates the potential for overload and conflict for dual-earner couples attempting to fulfil multiple demands. Stress audits can be carried out to detect symptoms and causes of pressure; and modifications made to work practices if necessary.

❚ The workaholic syndrome and the Type A behaviour pattern which are often associated with it are both counterproductive, producing behaviours associated with ill health and with relationship problems. Unfortunately, the workplace environment actually encourages these behaviours. It is important for managers to recognize this type of behaviour in themselves and others, and to atttempt to discourage employees from adopting these behavioural styles. Managers ensure that they themselves are not role models for stress inducing behaviour. Too often organizations do not question the value of workaholic behaviour until a key management figure suffers a heart attack.

❚ The long hours culture can encourage inefficiency and cause work–family spillover, stress and friction. Senior managers need to establish clear boundaries between work and family. Chief executives should make it plain that they want to spend time with their families and that they don't expect employees to spend all their time at the workplace. Remember, a balance between work and non-work is healthier for individuals and for the organization.

❚ Workloads are less likely to become stressful if employees have some control and autonomy over the number and flexibility of hours worked, and are able to modify work schedules without damaging career prospects. Chapter 6 considers this in more detail. For real autonomy to exist, there has to be an atmosphere of trust – managers must be confident that employees not working in the conventional time and place are nevertheless working conscientiously and efficiently. Autonomy breeds responsible attitudes to work to a much greater extent than autocratic systems.

The stress factors identified in this chapter, and the coping strategies adopted by those successfully managing work and family point to the need for training programmes in useful skills including time management, assertiveness and stress management. These are discussed further in Chapter 7. However, developing stress management skills should not be regarded as an alternative to addressing aspects of the workplace culture which create unnecessary stress.

3 Issues in Career Development

This chapter focuses on dual-career partners in professional and managerial careers. We look at some of the issues and dilemmas that they face (many of which apply just as much to other dual-earner couples), and some of the solutions they find. We also discuss steps that managers can take to assist employees in resolving these difficulties, so that they fulfil their potential and make a valuable contribution to their organization.

Preparing for a Dual-career Relationship

Career planning can be complex for members of dual-career couples. You have to take account of both partners' aspirations and to be able to integrate work and family life. Careers officers, teachers and others may offer advice on the choice and planning of a career: advice on planning for future family life and the integration of work and family is less easy to obtain!

You will need to discuss your aspirations in career terms, and also the implications of these aims on your relationship and your family life. Are both careers considered to be equally important, or will one career be given priority, either throughout the marriage or only at certain points in time? The implications of these decisions for choosing where to live and travel arrangements also need to be discussed. What will happen if your partner is required to relocate with his job? You also need to talk through such issues as *how* domestic work is to be shared, whether or not you want children and, if so, how you would cope with the extra demands of parenting.

Planning is much easier if you are realistic about their plans and about what the demands of work and family are likely to be.[1] For example, if issues about the importance of each partner's careers are not discussed initially, problems may subsequently arise when you discover that you have conflicting expectations from the relationship.

Making Plans, Being Flexible

A few of the couples we interviewed were very aware of the possible pitfalls and had developed highly detailed plans. For the majority, an agreement on basic values was considered to be sufficient. As one male sales manager suggested:

> I would say we didn't take any conscious decisions on day one. It just evolved but I don't think we'd have done it any other way. There were certainly no clear-cut plans, with dates set in concrete. But we did agree on basic philosophy from the outset and that is very important. Of course we argue about isolated incidents, but as long as we agree on the basics we can discuss problems and work things out.

Most couples emphasize the importance of flexibility and the ability to adapt plans, as it is impossible to predict every possible contingency. If either of you do not find jobs where and when you had planned or achieve your promotions, you may have to compromise on such matters as commuting, increasing travelling time or delaying or deciding not to become parents. So, agreement on basic principles is considered by most couples to be more helpful than the establishment of detailed, intricately worked out plans, as illustrated below:

> The key has been planning and organization and sometimes manipulating the system. Of course the plans haven't always worked out, so we had to adapt them. Perhaps when a job didn't come up in the right place and at the right time. Once I had to do an enormous amount of travelling so that Helen could continue her training. Being flexible and willing to adapt is important too.

Establishing Attitudes to Division of Labour

One of the most important basic principles which couples feel should be established concerns attitudes to domestic responsibilities. On a practical level, establishing who does what and who is responsible for what is important to avoid conflicts and misunderstandings at a later stage, as emphasized by this woman working in the computer industry:

> I would not do a lot different myself except for the old adage of start as you mean to go on. It's difficult to go back later. I often used to think 'blow it', I'll do it myself because I didn't like to bother him. Now if I have to ask him to do something it's considered an extra, whereas if we'd started off that way, it would be taken for granted.

It may be helpful in this context to 'talk through' attitudes to gender expectations, as your partner may feel guilty or uneasy about not conforming to stereotypes, as this paediatrician and mother of four illustrates:

> I still have the feeling that it's me who should be home for the children in the holidays or me who should be going to school events. I don't think mothers ever find it easy to get away from these feelings of guilt.

Despite women's increased involvement in careers and breadwinning, research over time and across cultures continues to document the persistence of inequality in the allocation of household work and in power relations within dual-career families.[2] When dual-career couples do move towards more egalitarian family roles, men more often share in the performance of domestic tasks than in the management of the household.[3] The household management role is a gender boundary which remains contentious and difficult to dismantle.

> Malcolm is very good. He helps with all the housework, washing and cooking. He'll do anything I ask him. (biologist)

The notion that a man's contribution to housework constitutes 'help' creates difficulty for some women, who feel guilty about asking for assistance, or angry about having to do so. One female manager blamed herself because she felt unable to ask her husband for help, even though she was quite comfortable in delegating and sharing responsibility at work, where the guidelines were much clearer:

> It's not that he doesn't want to help, I think it's something in me. If the roles were reversed I couldn't just sit and watch him make the dinner. I don't like having to tell him what to do. I'd like him to do it on his own initiative. If he just came and started preparing the veg I would be happy, but rather than ask him I do it myself.

Women's extra domestic responsibilities can create role conflict and overload and can spill over to affect women's experiences of work, reducing the potential for satisfaction and achievement in their careers. Continuing inequality is echoed in the workplace. Surprisingly, research indicates that dual-career women often report high levels of satisfaction with their partners' relatively modest contributions to family work.[4] Because domestic work has for so long been assumed

to be an essential part of the female role, women's expectations of their partners in this respect are often relatively low, and therefore any domestic or childcare work which men do share tends to be overvalued. This can lead to the superwoman syndrome,[5] whereby dual-earner women feel they have to perform to high standards both at work and in the home, which creates high levels of stress.

There is considerable evidence that women who earn as much as or more than their partners are in a position to negotiate greater husband participation in family work.[6] However, the significance of women's greater earning power is mediated by the various ways in which their income is defined. For example, women's income is often devalued subjectively, because it is perceived as expendable in the case of pressing domestic or childcare demands.[7] The way in which the value of a woman's income is defined by the partner's in terms of family financial support, is significant. Women who define themselves as co-breadwinners, rather than as generators of a second income, view their income as essential to family support,[8] and therefore feel entitled to equal consideration in domestic and career decisions. They are, for example, more willing to relocate for a better job than those who define their partners as the major breadwinners.[9]

Although women's greater earnings can alter family roles, they can also create tension as new expectations are negotiated. Gender boundaries in the family are most challenged when the woman earns more, or is more successful in career terms, than her partner.[10] The impact on the quality of the marital relationship as well as the woman's career is dependent on gender identity and expectations, particularly of the men.[11] Because men continue to feel that power and their masculinity are directly related to their role as a provider, this situation can be a threat to them. A female manager illustrated the problem when she described the problems created by her career success during her previous marriage:

> He resented my success and that I was more successful than he was. I earned more than him and consequently I had my independence. He resented that. He kept going on about my having affairs with people at work. It wasn't true, not for want of the chance but I wasn't interested. The more successful I became, the worse things were.

Some women respond consciously or unconsciously, by holding back in their career, in what they consider as an attempt to prioritize their family. A further education lecturer confessed:

> I could have gone much further in my career but I know that James would have felt the need to compete with me and there would have been murder at home. It wasn't worth it. My marriage is more important.

It may be useful to think through some of these issues, to discuss in advance what might be the response if one partner is more successful and how this can be handled.

Choice of Location

One of the first decisions to be made by dual-career couples is where you will live. This is usually determined by where you work. When both partners work in the same area there is no problem, but if you are each working or are offered jobs in different parts of the country, the decision about where to live becomes more difficult. With more 'traditional' couples this situation causes no dilemma, as it is accepted that even though the woman may be working the man's career should take precedence. When both careers are equally important, however, there is no tried and tested formula for dealing with the question of where to live. For some, it is possible to choose a location which is equidistant from both jobs, even though considerable travelling for both may be involved. For other couples, jobs are too far apart to allow commuting from one home. It then becomes necessary to work out a solution which will take account of the needs and aspirations of both partners.

Looking for Jobs in the Same Location

When both partners are entering the job market at the same time, it is usual to seek work in the same location, at least initially. Dual-career couples need to find two jobs, both of which will allow you to satisfy your own career needs and provide prospects for advancement. You will seek jobs that will enable you to live together and co-ordinate your schedules, to give yourselves some free time together and, if necessary, to fit in childcare. The task of seeking jobs which fit these needs can be daunting.

There are a number of job-seeking strategies which can be adopted by dual-career couples:

▌ The man locates a job first and the woman follows him. This is the traditional strategy.

▌ The woman locates a job first and the man then seeks work in the same area. This is non-traditional.

Neither of these strategies can be considered egalitarian, although they may work well in specific circumstances. A number of more egalitarian strategies can be adopted.

▌ Each of you looks for a job independently, and the couple choose the best joint option.

▌ You may both apply as a unit either to the same employer or in the same geographical area.

▌ You may apply for one job, that is, to job share.

▌ Each of you may accept the best opportunity available in any location, and then live apart during the week.

Stress and Satisfaction in Joint Job Seeking

The process of simultaneous job seeking for dual-career couples can be quite stressful. You may have to deal with issues of competition and power because, unless two suitable positions are readily available, one partner may have to accept a position at the expense of the other. This may lead to a sense of failure if you are unable to live up to their egalitarian ideals. The converse of this is that there is considerable satisfaction to be gained from joint job seeking, especially when problems are worked out. You may feel that you have proved yourself ready to make sacrifices in the interest of equality, and this may strengthen your relationship.

Choice of Locations when Both Partners are Already Established in Jobs

If both of you already have jobs at the beginning of your relationship you may face similar problems. Highly educated, career-orientated women tend to delay marriage until they are established in their careers. However, problems arise when both partners have established careers in different geographical areas. Strategies used to deal with this dilemma include compromise, alternating the location in favour of each partner, and commuting.

Problem solving and compromise

Although it is often necessary to give priority to one partner's career, you can reach a compromise on the basis of logical decision-making, rather than because of gender stereotypes (although the decision frequently upholds such stereotypes). A consultant physician explained that:

> My husband got his consultancy first so we moved and I transferred to a position here. He was offered posts in nicer places but chose to be in a large city so there would be more opportunities for me. Also, to be fair, there are fewer posts available in his speciality than mine and that had to be considered too.

It is possible that this logical approach is simply a way of rationalizing and justifying your decision. Nevertheless, it does appear that many couples are now considering all aspects of such a situation, giving equal weight to the needs of each career.

Alternating decisions in favour of each partner

When decisions about location are made in favour of one partner, it is often with a recognition that, if the occasion arises, decisions about further moves will favour the other partner. Often this decision takes account of the fact that one partner may wish to take a break for childrearing at some stage. A lecturer in business studies explains the dilemma she and her husband faced and the solution they reached:

> We were unusual, I think, because I would have said that normally one goes to where one's husband's livelihood is. He was working and living in Scotland and I was running a business here at the time and I didn't go there. He gave up his job and found one with a firm here. That was my condition, but of course it suited him too. We knew the decision may be different later.

Later in the marriage her husband was relocated. By then they had a young baby and the mother took a career break and moved with her husband. Dilemmas were thus resolved as they arose by alternating decisions in favour of each partner and responding to circumstances at the time.

Commuter Marriages – Living Apart Together

For some couples it is not possible to reach an acceptable solution which enables them to fulfil both partners' career needs and to live in the same place. Even if a compromise or a wholly satisfactory arrangement is reached, this does not guarantee that the problem will not recur. Many dual-earner partners who were satisfied with their original location decision, later felt constrained.

> We came here at first because I was working here, so Michael found a job here too. Then he accepted a partnership in the

firm of solicitors he was with and of course that is relatively permanent. Then I was very restricted. It would have been much easier to have progressed in my career if I could have looked for jobs elsewhere. I suppose I didn't consider working in a different town at that time. I have thought about it recently but now we have children it seems really impossible. I do feel frustrated because I have missed out on opportunities. (systems analyst)

My only problem is that if I want promotion I have to go to London and my husband has said that there is no way he will give up his job and go back to London. I think this is a major problem facing many couples. (manager)

These dilemmas illustrate once again the need to be flexible and to continually reappraise situations. Plans and compromises made early in marriage may become unsatisfactory or unworkable at a later stage. One solution to this dilemma is for you to live apart either during the week or for longer periods.

Research suggests that the success of this solution depends on a number of factors:

▌ *Age.* Commuter marriages work better for older couples who have had time to cement their marriages.

▌ *Children.* The problems of increased childcare responsibility for one partner complicate this arrangement for parents. Commuting is easier for couples who have no children or whose children have already left home.

▌ *Distance.* A relatively short distance between locations, enabling you to see each other regularly, is less stressful than distances which force long separations.

▌ *Conditions of employment.* Flexibility of working hours and the use of computers and other equipment for working from home can reduce the length of time you need to spend apart. Work that does not spill over into weekends is also important, so that you can spend your time together without pressures from work impinging upon you.

▎ *Income.* A high income is essential to maintain two homes, and this can also reduce strain by allowing frequent travel and telephone calls.

▎ *Lack of permanence of the arrangement.* Most commuting couples see the arrangement as temporary, although this is not necessarily realistic. Defining the situation in this way helps you to cope with separations.

▎ *Positive attitudes.* Couples who take pride in being able to commute to advance each other's careers, and who reaffirm the importance of being married, are the most likely to find living apart a satisfactory experience.

Living apart can threaten the sense of what marriage should be, and diminish your sense of security. You may feel depressed, lonely or resentful about each other's independence. Often a period of adjustment is necessary when you do have time together. On the positive side, it can increase your romantic attachment, equalize the division of labour and open new horizons for career advancement.

It is never an easy option, but one which may sometimes be preferable to the alternatives.

> When my husband moved to his new job I stayed on for the girls to finish school. I think that was the loneliest, most unhappy period of my life. The trouble was that I was too proud to admit it. Sometimes I would tell him not to worry about coming home at a weekend if he was very busy, but if he took me up on it I was devastated. (university lecturer, female)

Parenting, Careers and Mobility

Perhaps the most difficult decisions facing dual-career couples, and those intricately linked to career mobility and relocation issues, are about whether or not to have children and, if so, how to plan the timing of children to fit in with your careers. Often there is pressure from relatives or friends to conform to the prevalent view of a 'real' family by having children. Occasionally, there is also conflict between husband and wife on this issue:

> My parents and my husband think I should have a family by now. I have to choose between a career and children, it seems, or try to do both jobs inadequately. I haven't decided what to do yet. (senior technician, female)

Although the decision to have a child is normally taken by both partners, most feel that the implications tend to be greater for the woman. A woman manager who elected not to have children commented:

> I think it is the case for a lot of women that they have to make the choice between career success and family, and what really rankles me is that men simply don't have to make that choice. I feel they don't, because they put the burden on women.

Many women who do have children reduce their career involvement, temporarily, because of the difficulty in balancing career and childcare. It is still widely believed that mothers should assume the major responsibility for children, and this can create feelings of guilt in women who continue to pursue their careers while their children are young. It can be a struggle for women to convince employers that they are still committed to their careers while also conforming to the still popular notion of a good mother (one who is always there for the children). Even when fathers are eager to participate equally in childcare, it is often difficult for them to adapt their work for family reasons. Lack of adequate childcare provisions, together with long and inflexible hours of work, often make it difficult for both parents to work full-time. It is more often the mother who accommodates her career to care for children.

Not surprisingly then, fears of not being able to manage both motherhood and career, and anxieties about the constraints which motherhood will place upon career advancement, feature prominently in decisions and conflicts about whether or not to start a family.

> I would like to have a baby but I don't know how I would manage. I'd like to work part-time but that isn't possible with this firm. I might find someone else to job share with, but otherwise it just wouldn't work. (personnel manager)

Mothers who do return to their career after childbirth often confront prejudiced attitudes in employers.

> There is a lot of prejudice about women with young children in this organization. I'm really frightened that if I have a child it will ruin my chances of promotion. It's so unfair, nobody ever takes account of a man's family. (systems analyst)

Thus, dual-career couples often face considerable conflict. There may be pressure to 'conform' and start a family. Traditional attitudes to the roles of mothers and fathers often make this a difficult decision.

Delaying Decisions About Parenting

The recent trend is for women to delay having children. A common pattern in earlier decades was for women to enter or re-enter the labour force after their children were of school age. While there are still many women who shift to part-time work or take a career break until children start school, many career-oriented women feel that this will be career limiting.

> If you are trying to get back into the profession at the age of 40, there isn't much chance. This is the problem, the child-bearing years are the same years when you have to build your career. For a woman who drops out for a period of, say, five to ten years, it would be difficult to get back. You would be out of touch anyway. (chartered accountant, female)

Couples who delay parenthood until they are well-established in their careers often find that they have greater flexibility in managing competing demands. They are also more likely to be able to afford quality childcare. Many couples feel that waiting until the time is right is the ideal strategy.

> We both spent time working in hospitals and then we travelled a bit. Then we both found partnerships and spent a year moving into a new home. The time seemed right and we decided to have a baby. (doctor, male)

> We will wait until we can afford to have somebody to look after them, a nanny that is, before we think about children. I don't think there will be any problem if we can afford proper help. (radiologist, male)

Where career advancement is assured it is rational to delay having children. However, a crisis point occurs for many women in their 30s. At this stage they are often beginning to establish themselves in their career, but at the same time there is an awareness that time is running out for child-bearing.

Delaying parenthood is often a temporary strategy in the face of a difficult decision. Some parents maintain they never made an actual decision:

I think it's one of those things where you keep thinking I'll have children in a couple of years, but then by accident I became pregnant, so then you are faced with a *fait accompli*. (chartered accountant)

Other couples who put off having children until the time is right realize at some stage that it is too late.

Choosing Not to Have Children

Some dual-career couples make a deliberate decision not to have children. The decision involves weighing up personal needs, career issues and social expectations. Social norms which encourage childbearing can make the decision more difficult. In spite of this, a growing minority of women and men are questioning the inevitability of parenthood. For some the decision is very easy:

> The decision not to have children was never difficult for me. I just don't like babies. I never wanted all the hassle. If I could have given birth to a couple of teenagers that would have been great. Adrian knew this before we married. I was sterilized and have not regretted it. (university lecturer)

However, many people find this decision more difficult. There is often some conflict between the desire to have children and career ambitions. In these cases voluntary childlessness is often a choice made when the career-related costs of parenthood seem too high, particularly for women who also fear the loss of independence.

> I took a conscious decision years ago not to have children, because I was concerned about becoming dependent on somebody else's income, being constrained and not being able to seek my way in the world, in the way that men can. (insurance agent, female)

For some women the choice of childlessness may be interpreted as a protest against the heavy burdens which parenthood places on mothers. Many women report that in an ideal society they would like to have children, but that given current attitudes to mothers, lack of childcare provisions and the unresponsiveness of employers to parents, they decide to avoid what they regard as an untenable situation rather than attempting to modify it. This decision frees them from the burden of combining career and family, but ironically it does not always guarantee an escape from prejudiced attitudes. Some employers regard all women of childbearing age as potential mothers, and women who make known their decision not to have children are often regarded as deviant.

> You can't win really. The bosses think women with children are unreliable and lack ambition, but both male and female colleagues are suspicious of me because I don't intend to have kids. (public relations officer, female)

Planning for Children

If as a couple you decide that you do want children, the next decision to be made concerns the timing of pregnancy so as to take account of the career demands of both partners, especially the mother. For some couples children are regarded as a priority and careers are fitted around the family, rather than the other way around. This does not inevitably involve sacrificing professional opportunities.

> I had my children at various points during my training and career. The oldest was born while I was at medical school and the youngest after I became a consultant. You see, children are very important to me. I wanted a career too, but I didn't want to give up the chance of having a family. A lot of married women doctors delay having children. They pick the best posts, which might mean living separately from their husbands for much of the time. Then they wait to become a

consultant. Often they will have difficulty being appointed, because employers are suspicious of married women with no children. They think they will be going off on maternity leave as soon as they are appointed. And all the time these women's fertility is declining. I didn't know if I'd make it to become a consultant, so I had my family when it was convenient and I made it anyway. (consultant paediatrician with four children)

This woman was able to combine her two roles successfully, largely because there is a scheme for part-time training in the National Health Service for doctors and dentists with domestic commitments. For those in other occupations, especially where supply exceeds demand and there is fierce competition, this may not be so easy.

The Stress of Job Mobility and Relocation

Decisions about job mobility and relocation can be particularly difficult for dual-career families. You have to take account of factors such as children's education and social networks. Added to this, career needs of your partner can cause particular problems in dual-career couples.[12]

Relocating decisions, such as where exactly to live, tend to favour the man's career. It has traditionally been more usual and more socially acceptable for a woman to follow her partner than vice versa, and women more often feel that they should put their family's needs before their own. Also, despite progress that has been made in recent years men still earn more than women, on average. So if the man earns more you may decide to prioritize his career. For women in dual-career families, relocations can cause considerable frustration. A study of women managers in the UK found that the majority of those who were able to accept relocation were unmarried. Just under a quarter of all women managers interviewed were not mobile because of their partners' careers or because of other commitments.

Nevertheless a growing number of men are also refusing to relocate. Although women frequently accept constraints on mobility for family reasons, men have begun to do so only relatively recently. Consequently, there is still an expectation that men will be mobile (and that women will not be mobile, which can affect promotional decisions). Men who do not conform to this expectation are often regarded as lacking in professional commitment and their promotional opportunities may also be restricted. The constraints are nevertheless acceptable to men who value their family life and accept the importance of their partner's career. An engineer who accepted limited mobility, because his wife was a doctor in general practice, felt that there were sufficient opportunities for him within his geographical area. However, his involvement in childcare imposed further restrictions on him which he felt prospective employers had difficulty in understanding:

> I went for an interview recently and in the first few minutes after we sat down, the interviewer went over the three most important points. One was that I should be completely mobile; be free to work in London or Paris for a few weeks. I said no, I thought I had made it clear in my application form that I have a wife who is in practice here and I have a young child. I suppose they just assumed that my wife would take over.

Decisions by men or women to refuse jobs which require mobility or to resist relocation are by no means always easy. Even for couples who have considered the question in advance, making the actual decision can be very stressful, and for those who have to confront an unexpected situation it can perpetuate a crisis:

> When the organization I used to work for closed its northern branch, I was offered a position in London. The alternative was redundancy. It was difficult because Carolyn had a secure

position with the local authority here and, in fact, she earned more than I did. We talked about it a lot and considered the pros and cons. She didn't want to move and didn't think she could find an equivalent position elsewhere so easily. The stress of the decision-making caused us to argue a great deal and say a lot of acrimonious things we both regretted. Eventually, we decided to stay put. I was unemployed for nearly a year. I felt resentful, and I know she felt guilty. Somehow we survived and I found another position. (computer programmer, male)

The situation which this man described was stressful, not only because the refusal to relocate resulted in a period of unemployment but also because the decision had favoured his wife's career. It is not uncommon for women to have periods of unemployment before finding a position themselves after relocating in favour of their partner. However, couples who relocate on the basis of the woman's career often experience problems, because their behaviour contradicts 'normal' gender-appropriate behaviour.

A solution which many couples are seeking, and a few organizations are offering, is to relocate as a couple. This might involve both of you applying for new jobs in a given area together or one of you agreeing to relocate on the condition that the organization finds a suitable post, with no deterioration in promotion prospects, for his or her partner. This type of policy requires an enlightened and understanding attitude on the part of the employer, and may also involve considerable negotiation, planning and problem-solving on the part of the couple themselves. The tortuous processes involved in achieving such a solution are illustrated by the experiences of Kathy and Richard. The impetus for the move came from Kathy:

The college approached me about a year ago to ask if I would be interested in setting up a new department. They offered me a very attractive package which included the opportunity to work part of the time in the community, a car, a higher salary and relocation expenses. They also found a position for Richard. That was part of the package. Richard did not want to go, though. He's not as ambitious as me and he said he was happy in his present job. We talked about it for months and at one stage I was going to turn the job down. After all, what's the use of an interesting job if it ruins my marriage? My personal life is important, too. Eventually the college wrote to Richard stressing that they really valued his experience, and wanted him in his own right. After all, he is an expert in his field. After that he decided to go. There were some difficult times before we actually reached a decision that we would both move. (lecturer, female)

It appeared that Richard feared that he was being appointed as an incentive for his wife to move, rather than being valued in his own right. This fear was echoed by others in a similar situation. A female academic, younger and less professionally advanced than her spouse, voiced this opinion:

There were two posts available at the same university and we did think that we might both apply. I wasn't entirely happy about the idea because we would have presented ourselves as a package; we both come, or not at all. John already has his PhD and a lot more publications than I have, and I was afraid they might offer me a job in order to attract him and I wouldn't have been considered on my own merit.

As more men and women refuse to relocate, or agree to do so only as part of a package involving their partner, organizations may eventually be forced to recognize the realities of the dual-career lifestyle and take steps to make relocating decisions easier. However, it is likely that individuals committed to both career and family may continue for some time to be faced with dilemmas and tough decisions. There are ways, however, in which the dual-career couple may be helped to anticipate and deal with these problems.

How Can Managers Help?

▌ Dual-career partners can be encouraged to incorporate family decisions in career planning by, for example, career counselling and appraisal systems which acknowledge the legitimacy of non-traditional career paths.

▌ Recruitment and selection procedures can be adapted to meet the needs of dual earner partners involved in joint job seeking (see Chapter 8).

▌ Companies can modify their relocation policies and practice in a number of ways (see below).

Modifying Relocation Policies

1 For those individuals (and families) that need to be moved, organizations should provide the support required. This means help with buying and selling houses, helping partners find equivalent jobs, and allowing the individual and the family enough opportunities to familiarize themselves with the new location.

2 Organizations could consider gearing their relocation plans to an individual's 'home life' phases. It is obviously the case that at certain phases of a dual-career family cycle, change is less disruptive (e.g. when he or she is single) than at other phases (children beginning school, partner re-entering career). On occasions, moving a person may be inevitable and necessary (e.g. when an engineer possesses skills vital to a particular project), but in most cases any planned change could be considered in light of the individual and family circumstances, with a view to integrating them into the changes and demand of work.

3   The partner's role in the individual's job and career development has been almost ignored by employing organizations. It would seem reasonable that the partner should be given 'the option' to be involved in the decision-making and information-sharing process concerning any move that may impinge on the family.

At the moment, organizations are contracting with one element of the family unit, but making decisions which radically affect the unit as a whole. By operating in this way they often cause conflict between the individual and his or her family.

4   It is frequently the case that organizations provide their employee with inadequate notice regarding geographic moves. This usually involves them in a period of separation from their family, which may adversely affect them, their family, and in the long run the company, who may suffer from less efficient work performance as a direct consequence of the domestic conflicts.

5   The major sources of stress involved in any potential move stem from the uncertainty which is nurtured in organizations by misleading or often imprecise information about their career plans given to employees. Up to date, honest communications can only help to minimize the level of uncertainty about prospective developments and provide for greater acceptance and a smoother transition when it occurs.

6   The organization will have to reconsider its attitudes towards women executives. It will have to offer promotional moves to them on the same basis as male managers and will also have to provide women (and men) with the opportunities to refuse a transfer without damaging their promotional prospects or with

the same support facilities given to their male counterparts if they accept (e.g. helping to find their partner a job, temporary 'home help', relocation expenses, paying the differential on mortgage rates, etc). Implications for relocation are discussed further in Chapter 8.

This is a time of great social change, and corporate planners will have to be insightful, creative and innovative in designing effective strategies to deal with them.

4 Managing Transitions: The Transition to Parenthood

If you are a dual-earner family who has children, you will know that the transition to parenthood is a major life event which has a very significant impact on your career and experience of work. In this chapter, we consider some of the dilemmas facing new dual-earner parents, and discuss implications of these for managers.

Throughout everyone's life cycle there are major transitions to be faced: transitions from school to college, starting a new job, moving house, retiring from work and so on. Each of these major life changes requires us to learn new behaviours to fit into new environments, interact with new people and form new relationships. Every life transition involves some stress, but can also lead to personal growth and development, with opportunities for greater satisfaction if you can adapt successfully.

The Transition to Parenthood

The transition to parenthood is clearly a major, career-related event in women's lives, with maternity leave marking a *rite de passage*. The transition to new fatherhood tends to be considered less relevant to a man's career, but this also affects needs and behaviours at work.

The birth of a baby causes a major upheaval in family life. You have to deal with an enormous new responsibility and intense demands on your time, as well as further pressure caused by social expectations about the respective roles of mothers and fathers. Every so often a television programme or a newspaper article berates mothers for going to work and 'neglecting' their children, although (in this country, at least) we hear less of the need for fathers to spend more time with their children. This can make new mothers feel unnecessarily guilty. For professional and managerial women, the message that mothers ought not to be employed co-exists with the belief that educated women ought not to waste their opportunities by remaining at home, so they experience conflicting pressures. The situation is exacerbated in Britain by lack of public childcare provisions and paternity and parental leave provisions. For fathers, there is the expectation that work involvement should not be affected by parenthood, which can create difficulties for those who wish to adapt their work schedules to the needs of the family.

As part of our research programme we examined the impact of the transition to parenthood for dual-earner couples. We looked at pressures and symptoms of stress reported by 47 couples on two occasions: before the birth of their first child and again after the mother's return to work.[1] All the mothers-to-be planned to return to their jobs. After maternity leave new dual-earner parents, especially mothers, reported feeling increasingly pressurized by the multiple demands on their time. Many of them reported that they felt tired all the time, and at first they felt less satisfied with their lives in general than they had before the birth.

However, some rather surprising results emerged. A small subgroup of women decided not to, or were unable to, return to their job as planned after maternity leave. These women, and also their partners, were much more highly stressed and dissatisfied than the dual-earner parents. It seems that whether or not the mother returns to work, the transition to parenthood is inherently stressful in the short-term, but for mothers who plan to carry on working and for their partners, returning to employment actually *reduces* the strain of new parenthood. In fact, there is some evidence that mothers of young children, regardless of their career orientation, enjoy better mental health if they are employed than if they are not.[2] This may be reflected in their partners' well-being, balancing out the stress of the multiple demands of the dual-earner lifestyle.

Many of the couples in our study, especially those for whom childcare was not a problem, indicated that, despite the hectic nature of their lives, the dual-earner lifestyle enabled them to enjoy parenthood. As one mother put it:

> We enjoy the baby more because we are both working. If I were home all day I would be frustrated. It's nice to have someone to do the hard work. I just come home and play with her. I have the nice part.

The transition is rarely completely smooth, however. Most of the new dual-earner parents in our study identified problems or dilemmas, while a minority who worked in non-supportive organizations faced extreme difficulties.

Dilemmas and Issues for New Parents

Renegotiating Gender Roles and Relationships

The birth of a first baby is a major turning point in a marriage, often resulting in a decline in marital satisfaction and a trend towards a more traditional division of labour, even among couples who had previously enjoyed a very egalitarian relationship.[3] Couples who attempt to share 'parenting' as well as 'breadwinning' on an equal basis, have to construct and negotiate their roles in a social context, where the accepted norm is for the mother to take on the role of main *caregiver*, while the father merely 'helps'. This belief in the optional nature of the father's contribution to childcare (and the mother's contribution to breadwinning) is reinforced by the availability of maternity, but not paternity or parental leave, and by organizational expectations that new fatherhood should not affect men's work involvement.

During maternity leave, traditional gendered patterns of behaviour are often established which may continue when the mother returns to work. The more time the father is able to spend with the family at this stage, the more likely it is that the couple will be able to find a mutually agreeable and satisfying relationship as parents. In contrast, occupational demands which keep the father away from home for prolonged periods during this stage, can create conflict and dissatisfaction in the relationship. As there is evidence that marital dissatisfaction affects job satisfaction, this in turn can affect morale at work.

Returning to Work

New mothers often experience some misgivings when first returning to work and this may be reinforced by other people's reactions:

> Other women were horrified and asked me how I could leave such a small baby, as though I didn't love him. I felt very guilty. (designer)

> At first I used to tell people I was going back because I needed the money. I felt I needed to make excuses. But now I tell the truth. I came back because it's what I wanted to do. (teacher)

Although it is now much more common for new mothers to return to work after maternity leave, they are still sometimes criticized for doing so.

> when I told [my GP] I had plans for going back to work he said, 'You can't go back to work. If it was my wife she wouldn't be going back to work. You can't do that, you can't look after a handicapped child and go to work'.[4]

The main difference between women who fulfilled their plans to return to their jobs and other women in our study was age. Older women were more likely to return to work, having achieved more responsible jobs with higher incomes as a result of delaying starting a family.

This might appear to suggest that personal characteristics, especially career commitment, determine whether or not a new mother goes back to work, and hence there is little an organization can do to influence the decision. Not true! There are a number of reasons why women change their minds about returning:

▎ *Practical reasons.* Difficulties in finding suitable childcare are common. Practical solutions in terms of childcare assistance, extended career breaks and flexible working patterns all help to retain staff after maternity leave. Many women move to jobs which offer better conditions, such as job sharing or working from home.

▎ *Management structure and policy.* These can also influence women's attachment to their work, at all levels of the organization. Research has shown that a major factor determining whether women return to their jobs after maternity leave, is their perception of opportunities for women in their organization. In one study, new mothers, even in unskilled work, tended to return to their jobs if they were encouraged by their supervisors to think in career terms and to apply for promotions, and also if they could see other women progressing within the organization. In contrast, those mothers who saw no possibility of career prospects of any kind and who saw only men in the management structure, understandably saw no long-term impact in taking a break from full-time work, and were consequently more likely to change their mind about seeking reinstatement. Women who are frustrated in their career, because of lack of recognition or blocked promotions, may decide that a period of full-time motherhood offers a more satisfying alternative. A scientific officer, who did return to her job, illustrates this ambivalence:

> I love my work, but I didn't miss it while I was on maternity leave... to be honest I think I should have been promoted by now. If I was a man I would have been. If it seems that I'm not going to get anywhere I might consider giving up.

▌ *Financial commitments.* Sacrificing one income may not be a viable option, or your partner may lose his job unexpectedly.

Asking for More Flexibility

Should you ask for changes such as shorter or more flexible hours, or less travel (challenging the traditional male model of work)? Apart from financial considerations discussed above, career ambitions have to be balanced against family needs, so much depends on how you believe management will respond to your requests. In fact, few fathers in our study were entirely happy about asking for more flexibility, but equally many mothers did not feel that they could do so, or preferred not to be treated as what they saw as 'specials'. Women in very senior positions who may be the first to take maternity leave at their level, are often conscious of the need to 'set an example', dispel prejudices about the supposed unreliability of mothers with young children. Some respond by ensuring that colleagues suffer the least possible inconvenience. One husband explained about his wife, a partner in a firm of solicitors:

> I think the fact that Rosemary made the minimal conceivable disruption, rather than taking all the leave to which she was entitled, actually reinforces the fact that she was a reliable colleague. (company executive)

While colleagues may appreciate such efforts, it sets an expectation which other women may be unable to live up to. It is only by making known the needs of dual-earner parents that management awareness of these issues will be raised. Of course, there will always be some men and women who are happy to make no concessions to parenthood. There are many more, however, who would like more flexibility but who are reluctant to ask for this, lest it affects their career. Those who are able to combine work and family in a flexible way and remain highly competent, can force traditional managers to question the validity of traditional, rigid and often workaholic working patterns:

> I recently interviewed a woman and several men for an executive position. The woman told us directly that she intended to have another child and that she intended to leave the office at 5.15 prompt every day. This raised a problem. She was far and away the best applicant, but we work in an environment where it is rare for anyone to leave the office before 6.00 or 7.00. Also, we didn't know how we would cope with anyone in such a key position taking maternity leave. We talked about it and decided it was a weakness on our part if we couldn't accommodate the needs of someone who was such a good candidate. We took her on and have never regretted it. (company executive)

Reinstatement Problems

Although the vast majority of women in our study experienced no problems over reinstatement, there were nevertheless some employers who made it difficult or even impossible for new mothers to return to their jobs. At the extreme, three women were actually made redundant during maternity leave. Only in one case was this genuinely part of a large number of redundancies. Another, a 30-year-old computer consultant reported that as soon as she told her boss that she was pregnant, he made her life miserable. He made it clear that he did not want her back after she had the baby. As soon as she began her leave he appointed a replacement and when she was ready to return, she was told that she was redundant.

An equally illegal stance was taken by the employer of another woman, but this was even more surprising as the woman and her boss were both lawyers. She felt very bitter about losing her job with a firm for which she had worked for seven years, and although she took independent legal action and received a financial settlement, she did not feel that this compensated for the hurt she had suffered. While these cases are extreme, and clearly illegal, a number of less extreme and more common reinstatement issues were also reported.

Changes in the nature of the job

Approximately one third of the new mothers in our study reported that their jobs had changed in some way. There was a clear distinction between those women who were in control of the situation, negotiating change in their favour, and others on whom changes were imposed. The outcome was rarely satisfactory in the latter group. Many new mothers had been replaced permanently rather than on a temporary basis during their leave. They were then moved to another, often less interesting or less responsible job when they returned, and felt very demoralized.

> I felt that I was being shunted from pillar to post and no longer had a really useful role in the organization. (biochemist)

The decision to convert a temporary to a permanent replacement is often based on the assumption that a new mother is not likely to return to work. It may even be believed that if she does come back, she will not remain in her post for long, or may be less good at her job. Ironically, this attitude can become self-fulfilling: women who are given less challenging work often become disenchanted and confirm such suspicions by leaving their organizations:

> My boss just assumed I would not come back and trained someone new. I have been given a much less interesting job and quite honestly I am bored... I'm looking for another job now. (laboratory technician)

Women who were able to negotiate changes in their jobs usually did so to create greater flexibility. The most popular option was a period of part-time work to ease them back into their jobs and sort out childcare arrangements. Others made compromises in other respects, for instance, a nurse who arranged to do more night duty in order to spend time with her baby during the day, while her husband was at work; and an assistant buyer in a large store who elected to do more paperwork to reduce the amount of travel in her work. For these women, the compromises were considered worthwhile to enable them to sustain their careers and spend time with their children. The key point is that changes which are self-initiated are less stressful because you retain a sense of control.

Lilly Industries was one of the winners of the Parents at Work awards for the most family friendly companies[5] in 1996. One of the most popular aspects of its work/life programme is the *phased return to work after maternity leave or illness*. New mothers can select to come back gradually, with a period of part-time work before returning full-time.

Other policies include:

- paid paternity leave – maximum three days;

- career breaks (for those with at least five years service) – unpaid leave for study, childcare or eldercare;

- sabbaticals – agreed period of paid absence from work for study, childcare or eldercare. This is for a minimum of one month and maximum of one year;

- part-time work – between thirteen hours minimum and 20 hours maximum per week;

- reduced hours – fewer than full-time, more than 20 hours a week;

- job share;

- term-time only working;

- V-time reduced working hours for agreed period at reduced salary;

- staggered hours – flexible starting and finishing times, but not reduced hours;

- official homeworking – main place of work at home, plus shared work-station at Lilly location.

Lilly report benefits to the company in terms of staff retention, reduction on overheads and running costs due to flexible working, extended business hours and increased productivity.

It is widely assumed that any adjustments to the patterns of work after the birth of a child will be made by the mother. In some cases, changes are made by the father, either because his occupation is more flexible or because he wishes to spend more time with the child. For example, one of the new fathers in our study left his job as a designer because he believed that freelance work would give him the greater flexibility necessary for childcare. His wife continued in her full-time job, while he fitted in freelance assignments around childcare. For this father, as for many mothers, the birth of a child was a catalyst providing the opportunity to explore a new way of working. Motherhood, and to a lesser extent fatherhood, often acts as an incentive to career change.

Accumulation of work after maternity leave

Other women return to an increased workload. The nature of some jobs is such that it is difficult for a woman to be replaced during her absence. A tax inspector described her predicament:

> The nature of the job is such that work cannot be taken over by a temporary replacement, therefore I had two choices. One was to hand over all my cases to someone else on a permanent basis. The alternative was to keep all my files, so that in principle there would be no development on these cases for three months and the correspondence would just pile up.

She chose the latter course, although in practice she did a considerable amount of work during her leave so that the work would not mount up. She found this acceptable because it was her decision. Other women, however, believed that a temporary replacement could and, indeed, should have been appointed in their absence. Returning to a build-up of work, in addition to the demands of parenthood, can be highly stressful and is often unnecessary.

I had insisted on not being replaced permanently but did not expect not to be replaced at all. Nobody had done any of my work while I was away, so I had to catch up and keep up with the job and cope with a young baby. (civil servant)

Lack of support for new parents

While the couples in our study reported that many managers were willing to provide some practical support and flexibility, it appears that others were less sympathetic to the needs of new parents and created considerable extra pressure. This can be illustrated by two examples of unhelpful practice. In

Barbara is a VDU operator, employed in a large engineering company. Her husband, Ian, is a manager in another firm. Both work inflexible hours and Ian puts in many hours of overtime. Barbara returned to her job when their baby was six months old, partly, she says, for financial reasons and also because she enjoys her work and the company of her colleagues. Initially childcare presented a problem. There was no workplace nursery at either company and no affordable private nursery places available. It was decided that the baby would be looked after by Barbara's mother. This was not a very satisfactory arrangement as the grandmother lived a considerable distance away. Barbara took responsibility for transporting the baby to his grandparents' home, getting up at five in the morning to do some housework, taking the baby, and then usually arriving at work on time. Her supervisor was very insistent that Barbara should not 'take advantage' of the fact that she had a baby by arriving late. She was informed of this in no uncertain terms. No account was taken of her domestic situation and difficulties. Then she arrived five minutes late for work on two occasions in one week, and she was given a warning. She felt that rather than considering ways of helping her, the supervisor was implying that she should not really be working. The assumption that her work performance might suffer if she was occasionally five minutes late can be contrasted with the potential effect of this attitude on her work satisfaction and motivation. A satisfied worker who is occasionally and unavoidably late is likely to be more productive than a punctual and disaffected one.

both cases not only did management fail to support and encourage mothers back to work, but they created unnecessary difficulties, insisting that no concessions at all should be made to the parents' needs.

> Sally is employed in a large department store. John, her partner, is a surveyor. Sally returned to work when her baby was three months old and the couple took it in turns to take their daughter to nursery and to collect her after work. On two occasions when the baby became ill at the nursery, Sally was contacted at work. The nature of John's work made him more difficult to contact. The policy of Sally's firm was that if a member of staff was called away during the day, he or she must have written permission from two levels of management before leaving the premises. This unhelpful and rigid policy ensured that Sally felt uneasy about leaving her daughter if there was the slightest possibility of her being unwell, as she knew how difficult it would be for her to get away if there was an emergency.

In both these cases, it was the mother who bore the brunt of inflexible management policies. Such employers, typified by the cliché 'give them an inch and they'll take a mile', are suspicious of their employees rather than having an ethos of trust and a desire to assist staff in balancing their work and family contributions. Many of the fathers in our study also reported extreme difficulties, not only in being able to leave work in an emergency, but also in having to refuse overtime or otherwise restricting their work schedules in order to fit in childcare.

Much of the stress associated with the transition to parenthood for dual-earner couples originates from social expectations, stereotyped assumptions about parental responsibilities and unhelpful management practices. Nevertheless there are some managers and some organizations who are leading the way by doing much more than paying lip service to supporting dual-earner families. This is achieved by both informal and formal policies and practices.

Informal Policies – An Example of Good Practice

John is a training and development manager in a large company. His wife is a lawyer, with another company and they have two teenage children. He has always attempted to share parenting although over the years both he and his wife have sometimes encountered difficulties in balancing their careers with childcare and in negotiating a fair distribution of responsibility. John reported that these difficulties affect the way he regards members of his staff when they become parents.

He gave the example of Jane, a training officer, who came back to work when her baby was three months old. Bearing in mind his own experiences, he was concerned to minimize her difficulties, so he told her that when she was not actually involved in running courses there was no need for her to be in the office. She could, he maintained, be working just as effectively from home, where she could be contacted by telephone if necessary. Jane was grateful for this consideration, even though she mostly preferred to work in the office rather than at home. On occasions, however, such as when her baby or the childminder were ill, she did work from home if she was not involved in training. She did not abuse the 'privilege', but said that the knowledge that she could be more flexible, if necessary, made her feel more in control. She felt that her work and family responsibilities were manageable.

In this case there was no formal change in the overall organization, so parents elsewhere in the company may have been relatively disadvantaged. It demonstrates that awareness, and especially personal experience of dual-earner family issues, can change the ethos of a particular department, and hence the experiences of some new parents. However, the fact that there are men and women with family responsibilities in the management structure does not, *per se*, guarantee change. Indeed, we found some examples of parents who had progressed into management without making any personal concessions to the need for childcare, and who expected others to do likewise, often overlooking the less privileged positions of other parents. For instance, a tax inspector who was a mother of two, married to a teacher, and employing a nanny, said:

> I am fairly intolerant of women who take time off or who leave early because of their children. It gives other women a bad name.

The problem with this attitude is that it upholds the beliefs of the inflexible employer who does not recognize the difficulties which many people have when juggling their work and family needs. It is not enough to rely on the goodwill and understanding of individual managers: more formal organizational policies are also needed to ease the transition to parenthood. These are discussed in Chapter 8.

Summary and Implications for Managers

The advantages of facilitating the transition to parenthood. Becoming parents for the first time is a potentially stressful time for both men and women, but the evidence suggests that both parents find it easier to adapt if the mother is enabled to return to her job. Practices which make it easier for new mothers to get back to work and new fathers to have time for involvement in childcare therefore enhance the well-being of dual-earner employees at this stage of their lives. Obviously there are also advantages to employers in terms of maintaining organizational commitment, and retaining and motivating trained staff.

▌ *Management attitudes.* Good or bad practice in relation to employees' work and family experience stems from basic attitudes towards employees. These attitudes concern not only beliefs about gender roles and the ideal worker, but also fundamental management philosophies and trust or suspicion of workers. Some managers oppose more flexibility for employees because they do not trust them not to abuse these 'privileges'. However, trust or lack of it tends to become self-fulfilling.

▌ *Allow people to maintain a sense of control.* One of the major reasons why life transitions can be stressful is that they create a new situation in which individuals may feel that they have little or no control. New parents will adapt best when they are able to initiate the necessary changes in their work patterns. Employers should, therefore, aim to provide you with a sense of control. The changes parents most often want are those which make their jobs more flexible, enabling them to work out their optimum way of managing work and family.

▌ *Opportunities for women.* New mothers are more likely to return to their jobs and to be committed to the organization if they are encouraged to think in career rather than just job terms. This applies to all levels and occupations. Women who are encouraged to plan their careers, have role models of women in the management structure and do not encounter discrimination, will be most highly motivated and committed to the organization.

▌ *Encouraging alternative career paths.* Encouraging people to think in career terms does not necessarily imply that they must adhere to traditional career pathways of full-time continuous work. Employees can be encouraged to make long-term career plans which include periods of part-time work or breaks from employment. For alternative career planning to be a genuine option for men and women, several prevalent assumptions must be questioned. These include the widespread belief that career success must be achieved by a certain age. Career planning has to be seen as a flexible and lifelong process, with people progressing at different rates according to family needs, in a planned way, while remaining in control of their own lives. Appraisal interviews would be an appropriate place to look at these issues and make plans in the light of both individual and organizational needs.

Social support. The transition to parenthood is a potentially stressful period for new parents, particularly mothers, who still tend to assume greater responsibility for childcare. Adjustment to the transition is easier in the context of social support.[6] A generally supportive attitude from management makes it easier for parents to ask for concessions if necessary, and reduces the stress of uncertainty associated with possible unexpected occurrences such as illness of the child or child's carer.

Childcare assistance. Affordable, accessible, quality childcare is essential for working parents. In some cases workplace crèches are invaluable. We discuss various childcare options in the next chapter.

Training. As many of the problems involved in the transition to parenthood arise from a mismatch between social expectations concerning parenthood and paid work, training can play a vital role in challenging outmoded beliefs and ambivalence and providing alternative attitudes and strategies. It is important for training to be directed at managers and supervisors, who can be encouraged to reflect on dual-earner family issues and modify attitudes and policies accordingly. Training, especially combined with counselling, may be useful for prospective or new parents, enhancing personal effectiveness skills at work and at home. The case study below illustrates how this can be done.

Ikea have recently introduced a number of services for new parents and others with family commitments. The programme was developed by a voluntary organization, Exploring Parenthood, which was concerned about the stress associated with the transition to parenthood, the lack of equal involvement in parenting by fathers despite the growing employment rates of women with children, and the lack of support from employers for fathers to be more involved in consultation with Ikea management and staff. The programme comprises:

▌ A new parents programme. This is a two-year structured programme for pregnant staff and their partners. It offers support and follow up to enable staff to resume and sustain employment after childbirth. There is also information and help with childcare, to aid staff retention.

▌ An information and advice service on any matter, designed to ensure that problems experienced by staff, however minor, can be resolved before they escalate and disrupt work and/or family. This counselling can be provided on or off site, and is seen as integral to the company human resources and quality processes, rather than as separate problem or crisis management.

▌ A consultation service for managers and supervisors includes management training on work and family issues, advice to management on issues relating to maternity, childcare and other dependent care, family relationship problems, stress management and gender issues in the workplace. This service recognizes consultation as the best strategy for dealing with individual members of staff.

So by taking all these factors into account, employers can take steps to make transitions easier for both mothers and fathers – and for the company, too.

5 Workers Have Families, Too

We saw in the previous chapter that couples who continue the dual-earner lifestyle after becoming parents, may be less stressed than those who adopt a traditional single bread-winner structure. This is not to suggest, however, that managing two careers and the care of children or other family members is easy, particularly in the context of a traditional work ethic which assumes that family should not interfere with work, and a long hours culture. In this chapter, we discuss childcare and also eldercare-related issues for dual-earner families, and consider some initiatives which employers can take to facilitate the combining of caring and work demands.

The major pressures reported by couples in our survey who were combining careers and parenthood were:

- finding the time and energy to cope with the multiple demands;

- coping with conflict between demands; and (above all)

- the issue of finding satisfactory childcare.

Time and Energy

Balanced against the satisfaction of being able to 'have it all' expressed by most couples, was the problem of finding the time and energy to fit in the care of a young child with the demands of two careers. Exhaustion and feelings of 'not having enough hours in the day' were frequent complaints, particularly by women if fathers did not pull their weight. Generally, everything was fitted in, but at a cost and it was usually mothers who paid the greater price:

> I've felt tired for so long, it's just a part of my life since Alex was born. I had plenty of energy before. Now I just accept being tired. (nurse, mother of two-year-old son)

> I don't have time for me, to do what I want. I'm running around all day doing things for everyone else. I'm tired all the time and there's no time left to do the things I really enjoy. (manager, mother of a four-year-old son)

The demands on time and energy do not always decrease as children grow older. Nappies no longer need to be changed, but children have to be transported to and from school and to a host of other activities:

> I think life is rushed because of the children and all their activities and commitments. I don't think it's because of our careers that we are always rushed. (solicitor, mother of children aged 13, ten and two years)

The costs of combining two careers with parenthood should not be underestimated. Nevertheless most parents considered this to be worthwhile, as involvement in both career and family provides two sources of satisfaction.

Conflict

When people feel torn between the needs of children and the demands of work, the subsequent conflict can be very distressing:

If my child is ill and I have an important meeting at work I
have to decide which I should do first, take her to the doctor
or attend the meeting. I constantly feel torn in two directions.
(lawyer, female)

It is because work and family compete for scarce time and
energy that dual-earner parents are so vulnerable to role
conflict. Childless couples may also experience conflict
between work and family, for instance when faced with
relocation issues. However, although the childless couples
in our study reported some conflict between career and
family obligations, this was not a source of stress. For dual-
earner parents on the other hand, conflict was the major
cause of stress-related symptoms. Other research also
indicates that role conflict diminishes job satisfaction, life
satisfaction and mental health for dual-earner parents.[1]

Conflict between career and family tends to be greater for
mothers than for fathers, but men are not immune. A study
of professional and managerial men[2] revealed that conflicts
related to their workload or work-related travel interfering
with family life were common. However, it was men whose
wives were also employed in high-status occupations who
experienced the greatest level of conflict. The demands for
greater family involvement by men in dual-career couples
creates the potential for work–family conflict for fathers as
well as mothers.

Conflict between work and family is partly a result of
incompatible schedules, as discussed in Chapter 2. There is
also the conflict between what parents are actually doing
and what they feel that society expects them to do. This often
causes identity dilemmas, particularly for new mothers. The
prevailing definition of a 'good' mother in this country is
one who is not employed outside the home, or at least only
minimally, when a child is young.[3] This, of course, conflicts
with the social expectations about the good worker,
especially in managerial and professional work. The ideal

worker in this context is someone who does not allow family to interfere with work. So, conflict automatically exists.

> There is conflict. There is constant conflict. Perhaps it is my guilt. I think that is what causes the conflict. I'm sure my son isn't as worried as I am. He takes it all in his stride, but I almost feel that he's compartmentalized into one part of my life, which is something I don't want to happen. (manager, female)

> I think that all working mothers feel guilty about leaving their children. I feel guilty, especially about leaving them during school holidays or if one of them is ill. Sometimes one of them will say, 'Don't go to work today mummy, stay at home with me' and I feel awful. (paediatrician, female)

This guilt is often made worse by other people's comments:

> My biggest problem is my mother. She is very critical of me for working when the children are so young and she makes me feel very guilty about it. My two sisters both gave up work when they had children. Sometimes I have bad dreams about my mother dying and that increases the anxiety and guilt. (scientific officer, female)

Even women who reject the traditional female role may compare themselves and their performance at home as a parent, with full-time mothers. Inevitably such a comparison appears unfavourable, again fostering guilt and self-doubt:

> Sometimes I feel guilty and frustrated when I hear that my friends are doing such marvellous things with their children in the holidays – I feel my kids are missing out. (GP, female)

However committed women are to their job or career, they often feel they should spend more time with their children and conform to the popular view of a 'good mother'. At the same time women are also aware that life goes on beyond childrearing:

If it's a choice between my career and my son, then there's no choice at all. He comes first. But I'm also conscious that in ten years' time he will be probably going away to college and I might have missed the opportunity to make a successful career for myself. (manager, female)

Effects on Children

The guilt expressed by many career mothers stems from a belief that children really need exclusive maternal care during their formative years. It is appropriate at this point to examine the evidence for this view. During the 1950s, John Bowlby, a psychoanalyst, introduced the term 'maternal deprivation'[4]. He argued that separation from the mother can have devastating and long-lasting effects on the child's development. Bowlby's studies were based largely on children in institutions, whose total life patterns were disrupted and who were deprived of both mothers and fathers. He greatly underestimated the role of the father.

Certainly children do need to form an attachment with their mother and also with their father. However, the regular absence of their parents during the day while the child is cared for elsewhere, is in no way comparable to the situation of children in institutions or in hospitals. Maternal deprivation is too broad a term to be applied in a general way to all forms of separation. Nevertheless, Bowlby's work has had an enormous impact on society's attitude towards motherhood. Views on the acceptability of maternal employment have changed over the years, but the debate never quite disappears, and often emerges in the media or other contexts in response to a new piece of research (often wrongly interpreted) or some child behaviour for which a working mother can be blamed.

Concern about the possible impact that separation might have on children, led to a spate of research comparing the adjustment and well-being of children of employed and non-employed mothers. In most cases, research shows no overall differences between the two groups of children and several studies have demonstrated that the effect of maternal employment on children is, if anything, beneficial. There is no evidence that the children of working mothers are emotionally or socially deprived. Children of dual-earner parents benefit from greater paternal involvement and tend to be more independent and competent as a result of forming attachments to a number of people. Reviewing the research, Louis Hoffman[5] argued that children benefit from having a mother who is happy and fulfilled, whether as a full-time housewife or as a career mother. A bored, frustrated mother at home is less beneficial to a child than a stimulating nursery or a committed nanny, combined with the attention of parents in the evenings and at weekends. Children of homemaker mothers tend to have more stereotyped sex role attitudes, and daughters have lower self-esteem and aspirations than those of employed mothers; and evidence that high-achieving women and those in non-traditional occupations are more likely to be daughters of employed mothers attests to the value of a non-traditional role model for girls in particular.[6] A recent American study of adolescent daughters in dual-career, dual-earner and single-earner families[7] demonstrated that the extent to which the girls held non-stereotyped views of men's and women's roles and integrated these in their own self-concept, depended not only on whether their mother was employed, but also on the extent to which fathers were involved in family work. A non-traditional distribution of labour between parents, with substantial paternal involvement in the family, were most conducive to non-stereotypical gender roles and to a commitment to role sharing in the future that girls envisaged for themselves.

Boys too, seeing more equal power relations in the home, are less likely to develop rigid masculine sex roles. There is also evidence that maternal employment may be related to superior adjustment in adolescent children, probably because of the greater ease with which employed mothers can grant independence.[8] Finally, recent research has begun to ask children themselves what they feel about mothers working. Far from considering themselves to be deprived, or 'latchkey children', some as young as 10 or 12-years-old, report that they enjoy coming home, usually with friends, to a 'vacant' house in which they enjoy time to themselves.[9] Children can also gain satisfaction from their parents' work.[10] Clearly the anxiety and guilt experienced by some mothers, and the prejudiced attitudes of some managers, associated with the belief that children will suffer if both parents are employed, are misplaced. Nevertheless, children do report feeling less happy about their parents both working excessively long hours or at weekends and evenings.[11] This implies not that parents should not both work, but that they also need time away from work to enable them to lead balanced lives.

Childcare

Who is Responsible for the Children?

Childcare is the most time- and energy-consuming of occupations. Childcare, unlike domestic work, cannot be neglected. It is not possible to cope with extra demands by lowering standards, and children cannot be swept under the carpet – nor would you wish to do so. Professional couples expect their children to receive high-quality attention, but the burden of responsibility for providing this care often falls disproportionately on mothers.

Dual-earner families have evolved some way from the traditional family structure and childcare is more likely than domestic work to be shared equally. Almost one half of the parents in our study said that they shared responsibility for childcare equally, which demonstrates a growing awareness of the importance of fathering. However, half the couples still felt that childcare was primarily the mother's job.[12]

There are several reasons why dual-earner couples do not always share parenting equally despite commitment to non-traditional ideology.

Social expectations

The prevailing view that mothers are mainly responsible for the care and well-being of children is very influential. As discussed above, mothers feel guilty if they share childcare with fathers or others. The social expectation that fathers ought not to be as involved as mothers in early childcare is also widely voiced:

> Some people find it hard to deal with the fact that I am so involved in the children's upbringing. When I took the baby for his injections, the woman doctor asked me if his mother was ill. (community worker, male)

Traditional gender expectations

Men who conform to traditional masculine stereotypes by being highly competitive and power-oriented often feel that participating in childcare is too costly in career terms. Similarly, if you are one of those women who conform to the traditional female role you may be reluctant to relinquish the major responsibility for childcare.

Lack of role models

Many dual-earner spouses reared in traditional families are aware of a lack of role models for shared parenting:

I never saw my father really involved with his children, so I think it's been a slow and painful learning experience for me. (social worker, male)

The impact of maternity leave

The availability of maternity leave, but not paternity or parental leave, may play an important role in shaping patterns of parenting.

Obviously I did most of the work while I was at home, the nappies, the washing and so on. We just seemed to carry on that way after I came back. And the baby seems to respond better to me. After all I have been there all the time from the beginning. (personnel officer, female)

Organizational constraints

Managers and colleagues are often critical of men who wish to reduce their involvement in work to make time to be with their children. A more socially acceptable pattern is for fathers to work harder, putting in more overtime, when there are children to support. This 'breadwinner ethic' reduces the time and energy that fathers have available for childcare.

The Advantages of Shared Parenting

Men are increasingly participating in their children's care, particularly when mothers' schedules are either longer, or just different from those of the father.[13] The achievement of a more equal distribution of childcare responsibility is not only desirable on the basis of fairness. There is also much evidence that paternal involvement in childcare benefits mothers, children and fathers themselves in a number of ways:

▌ Dual-earner mothers obviously benefit by being less overloaded.

▌ Infants whose fathers are very involved in their care have been found to be intellectually and socially more advanced.[14]

▌ Several studies of dual-earner families indicate that fathers who are involved in childcare enjoy better mental health than their less participative counterparts.[15] This may be because there is less pressure from their wives and an improved marital relationship.

▌ Many men also feel that they gain from their close relationship with their children.

Fathers who play a full part in childcare generally consider the rewards greater than the sacrifices, although these sacrifices can be quite substantial. Participant fathers interviewed by Lucia Gilbert,[16] were often prepared to limit their professional aspirations or to lengthen their timetables for achieving their goals. Mothers frequently do just this. Other fathers make smaller sacrifices but this also benefits the family:

> It stops me being as free as I might be at weekends, but I don't mind. Colleagues who don't have a working wife might go and play golf. I know I would get it in the neck if I did that. That's part of the contract, if you like. (company executive, male)

Who Cares for the Children When Both Parents are at Work?

Making childcare arrangements can be a major source of stress for new parents. Being a working parent is not an easy thing to do; you may have to compromise, adjust your working hours, work part time, even change your job, to fit in with the needs of your child and employer. You don't want to leave your child with just anyone, so finding good, reliable and affordable care for your child is the key. In countries where it is normal for mothers of young children to be employed outside the home, childcare poses no problems. Nursery places are more widely available and affordable. In the UK pre-school childcare facilities are inadequate.[17]

Why is Finding the Right Kind of Care Important?

Childcare arrangements have an important impact on parents' experiences of work and satisfactory provisions help to protect against the pressures of the two-earner lifestyle. You can only begin to derive satisfaction from your job if you are first satisfied with your childcare arrangements.[18]

Getting the right care, that is flexible enough to meet your needs, and at a price you can afford, takes lots of planning and organization. Finding out the availability and cost of childcare in your area takes a lot of time and effort, and how can you be sure that the care you are offered is good and reliable? It will not help your career prospects by having to take time off because of a crisis with your childcare arrangements. Unstable arrangements will mean your worrying about them 'holding up' rather than concentrating on your job.

If you are lucky enough to have an employer with family-friendly policies and practices (be warned – there is often a large gap between policy and what actually happens), like flexible working times, additional leave for crisis, access to phones for personal use etc, which take into account family commitments, then combining caring for a family with employment may be *easier*, but it is never easy. There are almost no formal childcare arrangements or suppliers which can cope with unusual hours, for example shiftwork or emergency 'on call' types of jobs. Most childcare is geared to '9 to 5' working patterns and *you* are the one who has to make the adjustments to fit in with their hours.

The Major Types of Formal Childcare Available in Britain

Nanny – live in	Private nursery	Out of school club
Nanny – daily	Local authority nursery	Registered
Holiday playschemes		childminder

This is not an exhaustive list, and there are bound to be local variations in what is available. In rural or inner-city areas there is often a dearth of facilities due to 'low demand'. There are either not enough working parents, or they cannot afford to pay enough, to make childcare provision viable.

Pre-school Children

A choice made by many couples with a sufficiently high joint income, is to employ a nanny or what is known as a 'mother's help' (the very term indicating where parental duty is assumed to lie!) either on a live-in or a daily basis. Opinions are divided as to whether living-in help is acceptable:

> We wouldn't have a nanny living-in. There's no privacy. (physician, female)

> I think we will have somebody living-in until they [the children] leave school. Boarding school is definitely not the answer. The holidays are too long. (company executive, male)

Sometimes the decision to employ living-in help is reached as a last resort, after problems arise with other forms of childcare:

For the first child we had a series of arrangements. A childminder, then a nursery, but getting the baby out in the morning was such a rush. Then we had a series of people in on a daily basis and they kept leaving. When our second child was born, we gave in and employed a living-in nanny. It has made life much easier. (physician, female)

We found that parents who employed a nanny or other home-based help were less stressed than those using other forms of childcare. Nevertheless, many parents used child-minders or nurseries, not only for financial reasons, but because they believe they provide opportunities for inter-action with other children. A major difficulty with nurseries, however, is that the hours do not always coincide with parents' schedules. This problem can be resolved when a crèche is provided at the workplace of one of the parents. Those members of our survey fortunate enough to have such facilities generally found this very satisfactory.

The hospital nursery is indispensable to our way of life. (radiologist, female)

It was upsetting at first leaving the baby at the nursery, but I was lucky I was able to take him in and stay the first couple of days and gradually reduce the time I stayed over a period of weeks. And Jane can pop in during the day and see him. (salesman, married to nurse tutor using hospital nursery)

Given the lack of affordable childcare provision many couples rely on relatives to provide daytime childcare, but although this can be very satisfactory it is not always forthcoming and in some situations it may cause a strain on family relationships.

My parents used to look after the baby, but I found we disagreed about a lot of things. I could tell someone else how I wanted him to be raised but it wasn't easy to disagree with my parents – especially as I felt indebted to them. (computer consultant, female)

Finally it should be noted that when parents, especially mothers, describe the advantages of various types of pre-school childcare arrangements they are often very defensive. For many mothers of young children there is still an apparent need to justify the use of any substitute childcare:

The other two weren't as small when I left them. Perhaps I felt a bit guilty in those days, but now I realize that the baby is quite happy. It doesn't matter as long as you can trust the person you leave them with. Even women who don't work spend a lot of time going out shopping playing golf or going to coffee mornings. (solicitor, female)

School-aged Children

Once children start school, women who initially felt uneasy about continuing their career begin to feel more comfortable and indeed many women do not return to work until this stage. However, there are new problems as school hours do not fit in with the hours of most full-time employment. You may have to reorganize your lives so that you, or someone else, can collect the children from school:

It's much more difficult now she is at school. She has to be picked up at 3.30. The childminder was much more flexible. I could collect her at 5.30 or 6.00 (theatrical agent, female)

The growth in after-school clubs in recent years has made life much easier for working parents with school-aged children, but of course, these are not accessible in every area. Details of the Kids Club Network can be found at the end of this chapter.

As well as the time between the end of school and the end of the working day, school holidays also create a problem, so new arrangements must be made. Some schools run after-school programmes and various playschemes and camps exist for children in the holidays. A few employers also help with this sort of provision. For example, Midland Bank runs holiday play schemes for school-aged children in many regions.[19] Some useful addresses are given at the end of this chapter.

Parents may also face difficulties in living up to the expectations of teachers and schoolchildren. Again the pressure to meet these expectations is more often experienced by mothers, although many fathers are also aware of the problem:

> Sometimes it's a problem when the children have to have a fancy dress for school. I mean there just isn't time to make elaborate fancy dresses like other mothers do, so I feel my kids miss out. (paediatrician, female)

> There are events at school to which parents are invited, often at short notice. It's difficult for either of us to be there, but we do try our best if we have time to arrange things, because we know other children will have a parent there. (dentist, male)

In part this problem arises because schools' expectations of parents' availability may be unrealistic. It can also be argued, however, that there is a justifiable expectation that jobs should be more flexible in order to allow parents the space to have some involvement in children's school lives. There should be an element of 'give and take' between schools and employers.

Who Stays at Home in a Crisis?

Even if there are well-organized, regular childcare arrangements with back-up systems, there is always the potential for something to go wrong. If your child is too ill to go to nursery or school, the nanny or babysitter is ill and friends and relatives are just not available, it may be necessary for one parent to remain at home. The question then arises, who is going to cancel appointments or interrupt their work?

We asked dual-earner parents the question 'Who would be more likely to take time off work in a domestic crisis?' Just under 30 per cent responded that it would depend upon which parent was most busy at work and 7 per cent said it would be the father. Over 60 per cent of couples maintained that the mother would be the one most likely to take time off. So when childcare crises arise the father's work life is much less likely to be disrupted than the mother's, thus reinforcing the stereotype of working mothers as 'unreliable'. Social expectations clearly play a large part in perpetuating this situation. It is often difficult for men to take time off without their professional commitment being called into question. However, many women are determined not to allow children to interfere with their work at any cost, for fear of being seen to conform to the female stereotype:

> I feel that I have to work harder and perform better than male colleagues or colleagues without young children. It's as though I am on trial. There is no way I could take time off if one of the kids was sick. It would just reinforce the general prejudices. (product manager, mother of two)

Schools and nurseries also play a part in reinforcing this view of the mother's responsibility for children. If children become ill at school parents must be contacted. It is a frequent complaint that although both parents leave their telephone number in case a child becomes ill, it is invariably the mother who is contacted first and who must disrupt her work:

> The school has both our numbers but if Jonathan is ill they always phone me. On one occasion I was in a lecture and found a message when I returned to my office. I phoned the

school just to check that they had managed to contact my husband but they hadn't even tried. The secretary said she didn't like to bother him. The really infuriating thing is that my husband is a school governor and they think nothing of contacting him if the roof is leaking or something like that, but not because his child his ill. (lecturer, female)

Social policy also mitigates against fathers taking their share of work disruption due to childcare crises. In the UK there is no national provision for paid sick leave to take care of a child, although some organizations do provide this facility. Unpaid leave is more likely to be taken by the mother except where she earns the higher income, both because it is more socially acceptable and it would be less costly. If paid leave were available for either parent this might legitimize the taking of leave for family reasons and lead to greater equality in terms of which parent stays at home.

Despite the powerful influence of social expectations, many men do take an equal, or even greater share of responsibility for dealing with childcare crises. For people who are highly committed to their careers, it is rarely an easy decision to drop everything and stay at home, but neither is it always easy to leave a sick child. When both parents have busy schedules, a crisis of this nature can cause considerable conflict. A psychologist and mother of two described how she and her partner had attempted to deal with such a contingency:

This is something we planned and talked about – the potential conflict between our jobs if the children were sick. We arranged that we would just divide the week into two without any arguments. If a child was sick and someone had to stay with her in the first part of the week, then one of us would take time off, irrespective of what was going on at work and vice versa for the second half of the week. In practice of course there was more discussion on individual days, because some days one of us would have very little to do and it would be silly to be inflexible. But it did mean that in principle if one of us didn't have a lot pencilled in our diary on a particular day, we weren't obliged to be the one at home. And it avoided arguments about whose work is more important.

An important point made by many parents, is that childcare crises are just that – crises, by and large, do not happen frequently. In the normal run of events, parents' working time suffers the minimum of disruption, although as with employees' own illnesses, crises are unpredictable. Even in quite difficult circumstances, however, dual-earner parents usually manage to cope, often much better than their employers expect them to do. This is illustrated by the case of Julia, a solicitor in a large organization and Graeme, also a solicitor, who have a disabled child. Julia's employers anticipated that this would cause particular disruption to her career and were sympathetic about this, but as she explained, they were mistaken:

> I have a mentally handicapped child and worry about him a great deal. This doesn't have to interfere with my work though. I find that the more responsible and onerous duties are not asked of me, partly out of a misplaced sense of kindness and over-protectiveness on the part of my superiors and partly, I suspect, because I am not expected to be reliable.

Disabled Children

Combining dual careers with the care of a disabled child can present even more issues. You need flexibility to be able to attend hospital appointments and appointments with health professionals as well as coping with the child's hospitalizations or other emergencies. Furthermore, unlike parents of children without impairments, you have to provide care on a much longer term basis, and often for the rest of their lives. Nevertheless, with the right supports (childcare and flexibility at work, and formal and informal support in the community) parents can sustain a career and provide care, and tend to be less stressed than parents who care full time.[20]

Additional Dilemmas Facing Lone Parents

The position for lone parents is even more difficult than for dual-earner couples. Because they have to cope alone the (almost exclusively) mothers have to find work which provides considerable flexibility. You can do this, but at a cost, for example, self-employment may give you time to care, but provides a precarious income; part-time work is fairly flexible but poorly paid. Family Credit helps, but as a lone parent you may find you are then unable to move out of the 'trap' of low-paid work.[21]

As a lone parent you have no partner to share the care with, which often necessitates the purchase of more formal childcare than two-parent families. You may have more restricted social networks, and being less able to reciprocate favours and support, feel uncomfortable accepting them.[22]

Getting Information on Finding Reliable Childcare

This very much depends on the age of your children, what hours/days you need childcare, what kind of childcare you are looking for and how much you can afford to spend.

The Rolls Royce option, which gives you the greatest flexibility, is a Nanny. Nannies can be live-in, freeing you from having to be home at a specific time to pick the children up, or daily. The usual way to recruit a Nanny is through an employment agency (note: they are now deregulated). To ensure that the agency is a reputable one, a good starting point would be to choose an agency which is a member of the professional association for employment agencies, The Federation of Recruitment and Employment Services (FRES), which has guidelines for agencies and information on employment contract for Nannies.

Contact: *FRES, 36–38 Mortimer Street, London.*

Nurseries, both public and private, can be found through the Local Authority Social Services Department. Anyone looking after children under eight years old has to be registered with them under the terms of the Children's Act. But you must be aware that not all nurseries are open for working hours; most Local Authority nurseries/nursery classes (start at 3–4 years old) are time limited (two and a half to six hours per day), so make sure your choice can cover the hours you need, whether it can cope with the occasional variation and has policies about what to do in a minor crisis – other than ring you at work to come and sort it out.

Similarly, childminders should be registered with and checked by the Local Authority. For a free Information pack on childminding which should be of use to parents, employers and prospective childminders, send an A5 SAE to: *National Childminding, 8 Masons Hill, Bromley, Kent, BR2 9EY.*

Out-of-School Clubs are growing rapidly in number. They provide a safe, stimulating environment where school-aged children can be cared for after, and sometimes before, school hours. Often based in a local school, or providing transport from school to the club, they have trained staff to look after the children and usually provide a meal of some kind.

For more information on the clubs, where they are to be found and even how to start one, contact: *The Kids' Club Network, Bellerive House, 3 Muirfield Crescent, London, E14 9SZ* or their Information Line 0171 5122100.

Holiday playschemes. Where there is a Kids Club you will find they often organize playschemes, if not contact the Local

Authority for information on any schemes in your area. But beware – there are often age limits on the children they accept, their hours are often restricted to even less than school hours and not all of them last the whole of the school holidays, or even take place during some of them.

How Much Will Childcare Cost?

Finding good quality, reliable childcare which meets your specific needs is very difficult and costly. The Daycare Trust, in their briefing paper 'The Childcare Gap', summarize the available formal childcare options and their costs (see Table 1 over the page).

Getting Help with Childcare Costs

Help with the cost of childcare is only available to working parents if you are on a low income and entitled to claim Family Credit. At present there is the Childcare Disregard, where up to £60 per week of family income can be offset against childcare costs (for children _under 11 years_) _per family_, when calculating Family Credit entitlements, provided a registered childminder, out-of-school club or other formally recognized service is used. The Childcare Disregard is also available to parents on means-tested benefits such as Housing Benefit, Council Tax Benefit and Disability Working Allowance.

Some employers offer help with finding or paying for nursery places, but this is not a very frequent 'perk' and is very much on an _ad hoc_ basis, even though employers can get tax relief on the costs of providing care or paying allowances. Generally speaking, finding and paying for childcare is your responsibility. Where an employer pays for childcare the employee does not pay tax on this as long as their employer is 'wholly or partly responsible for financing

Table 1 *Costs of childcare (guide)*

Age group of child	Type of care	Cost: per child : per week (Mon–Fri)	Duration of care provided
Pre-school	Private nursery	£70–180	Full time place
Pre-school	Registered childminder	£50–100	Full time
[1]Any age	Nanny (live in or daily)	£80–260	Full time but hours vary
[2]School age	Out of school club	£15–30[3]	After school usually 3–6pm[4]
School age	Registered childminder	£25–50	After school
Any age[5]	Playscheme	£50–80	School holidays

Source: The Daycare Trust

Note: There will be variations in costs and availability in different regions of the country.

1. For children under three years different costs/arrangements may sometimes need to be made. Source: 'Universal Care' employment agency, a member of The Federation of Recruitment and Employment Agencies (FRES).
2. Usually Secondary school.
3. Kids' Club Network say latest figures are from £18/week but, on an individual club basis, will try to vary this if there is a specific need.
4. Note: sometimes before-school care is available, but at additional cost.
5. Ages of children accepted may vary, check locally.

and managing the provision'. This means, in practice, workplace nurseries and out-of-school schemes.

If you receive childcare vouchers from your employer (which cannot be exchanged for cash), then National Insurance is waived for both employers and employees on this payment.

Fee Direct is a scheme in which part of an employee's annual remuneration package is reallocated into direct payment of childcare costs, ie your salary is reduced. This

Case Study

The cost of childcare for a family with two children aged 2½ and 7, living in Coventry, where both parents work full-time is calculated as:

During term time (39 weeks)

Private nursery place for the 2-year-old   £80 per week .... £3120 per year

Out of school club for the 7-year-old   £25 per week .... £975 per year

During school holidays (13 weeks)

Private nursery place for the 2-year-old   £80 per week .... £3120 per year

Holiday playscheme for the 7-year-old   £60 per week .... £780 per year

Total spend on childcare   £5915 per year

Source: The Daycare Trust

results in a reduction of both your tax and your National Insurance contributions. At present this scheme is negotiated on a local basis between employers and Inland Revenue Offices.

The last Government introduced Nursery Vouchers in trial areas to provide parents of four year olds with £1100 to spend on nursery schools or reception classes (the latter are *free* at the moment in most areas), or in playgroups or nurseries. The amount available under this scheme would pay for about two or three hours per day, five days a week for 39 weeks a year (term time only) but at the time of writing it is unclear whether this or a similar scheme will be extended nationally.

Changes Likely to Take Effect in the Near Future

The Kids' Club Network are presently working on a scheme, with the Luncheon Voucher Group, to introduce childcare vouchers which could be used to purchase care, an easier way for employers to contribute to employees' childcare needs.

From July 1998 the Childcare Disregard will be rising to £100 per week; £60 for the first child and £40 for the second child *under 12 years*, an increase in the Childcare Disregard available and a one-year change in the age limit.

In the recent 'Green Budget' the Government announced there would be £300 million made available for out-of-school clubs and £200 million for homework clubs. This *may* change the availability, or cost, of care for school-age children but there is no precise information as yet on exactly how the money will be distributed.

How Can Organizations Help?

Childcare Provisions

Below we discuss some of the options available to organizations to alleviate employees' childcare problems. Some of these benefits are offered by a small, but growing, number of organizations in the UK or elsewhere.

Workplace nurseries

Traditionally, workplace nurseries have been provided in organizations such as hospitals, which employ large numbers of highly trained women and recognize the importance of accommodating their childcare needs. More recently the need for such facilities has been recognized in a wider range of organizations. Unlike other forms of childcare provision, workplace nurseries are not taxed as an employee perk. This applies whether they are on- or off-site and also to nurseries run jointly with other companies, or with local authorities, providing that the premises are made available by one or more of the participants, and the employer providing the exempt benefits is wholly or partly responsible for financing and managing the provision. The cost of setting up and running a workplace nursery is often considered to be prohibitive but this should be seen as a benefit in kind similar to, and equally essential as, a canteen or sports and social clubs. Furthermore, workplace nurseries have been shown to have economic as well as qualitative benefits. Savings are calculated in terms of recruitment and retraining due to the dramatic rise in the number of women returning after maternity leave, as well as the benefits of reduced stress, decline in absenteeism and improved timekeeping.

Among the employers providing workplace nurseries is Midland Bank, which began its nursery programme in 1988 and now has over 115 nurseries in locations around the country, providing places for approximately 850 children of employees. The nurseries are open to children of full- and part-time employees. Quality of childcare is constantly monitored to ensure that standards are upheld.

On-site childcare or a nursery located very near to the place of work has several advantages over other forms of childcare:

▌ Parents can see their children during the day and are readily available in an emergency.

▌ Crèches are invaluable for mothers who return to work while still breast-feeding.

▌ The hours of a workplace nursery obviously coincide with those of the working day, avoiding the problems of incompatible schedules.

On-site childcare makes life much easier for parents and this is reflected in improved performance and satisfaction, a better working climate and lower turnover. Despite these substantial benefits, however, there are also limitations to workplace nurseries. Employees who commute long distances to work may prefer a childcare facility nearer to or at home because of the hassles of travelling with the child. Clearly workplace nurseries can be invaluable under some circumstances, but in other situations, such as when a company draws personnel from a wide range of locations, it might also be worthwhile considering other related options.

Childcare consortia

Many employers reject the notion of a workplace nursery on the grounds that the number of employees with young children is too small to justify such a provision. However, the need for childcare still exists for parents employed in smaller organizations. One strategy is for an organization to set up a nursery, giving priority to its own employees while also providing places for employees of neighbouring companies, who would contribute to the cost.

Another way of increasing demand and spreading the cost, is for a number of employers in close proximity, or drawing from a workforce in a common residential area, to form a consortium to share the provision of a nursery.

Working with local government

The number of state nurseries has declined dramatically with recent cuts in public spending. The business community can work together with local government by contributing funds to enable established nurseries to remain open or those which have been forced to close, to re-open. When planning permission for a new office development on behalf of Merrill Lynch stockbrokers was sought, the local council, Islington, required that childcare facilities should be included as part of planning gain. The result was the opening of the City Child Nursery in January 1988, in the heart of London's financial centre. The pooling of local authorities' childcare expertise and private sector financial resources may well lead to other joint ventures of this nature.

Other financial benefits

A growing number of organizations in Britain now provide employees with childcare allowances. Direct financial contributions towards childcare, or Childcare Vouchers, although taxable, increase parents' choices. Money or vouchers can be used to fund a nursery place or childminder, or as a contribution towards the cost of a nanny, or paying a relative. Alternatively, some employers contract with existing private childcare facilities, offering discount on childcare fees to their employees. Arrangements include subsidising 'slots' of places in a nursery. Employers guarantee payment for a number of places and these are reserved for company employees.

Other firms operate a voucher system. This is a subsidy provided by the organization to its employees to enable them to purchase childcare from any recognized nursery or childminder. In some types of work parents may be required to work extra hours at certain times, which can make childcare arrangements difficult or expensive. Some employers recognize this by paying extra childcare costs when this occurs. For example, Nottingham Hostels Liaison Group, (HLG) a small voluntary sector organization with 20 employees which assists homeless people and the hostels and projects which accommodate and support them pays care costs for childcare or other care which may be disrupted by extra working time. Where a member of staff who is a parent, or regular carer, or primary carer of an adult dependant is required to work extra hours in the daytime, weekends or evenings, the costs of additional childcare or other dependant care are paid.

In addition to providing childcare on-site and/or assisting with off-site childcare for the under-fives, there are a number of other ways in which organizations can reduce stress for dual-career parents.

Information and referral service

New parents or parents newly resident in a particular location can benefit from a service providing information about local childcare services. This includes lists of nurseries, childminders and agencies providing nannies and other in-home help. Several organizations have found this to be a relatively inexpensive but nevertheless valuable service. For example, Price Waterhouse has an on-line childcare database accessible from each work station, and a booklet on 'Planning your Childcare', with guidance on planning, options, choosing childcare and crisis management. In 1996 it introduced childcare vouchers, based on a proportion of salary at the time of the mother's return to work, for a period of 12 months.

Childcare co-ordinator

Some organizations such as Allied Dunbar in the private sector, and the Royal Borough of Kingston in the public sector, employ a childcare co-ordinator to help employees to locate and arrange the right sort of childcare.

Paid leave to care for a sick child

It is imperative that organizations formulate a policy on sick children, to complement childcare policies. Most European states have legislation granting employees the right to some paid leave for pressing family reasons. Britain has yet to act on this matter. Nevertheless a few organizations do provide paid leave for a specific maximum period to care for a sick child. If this benefit is made available to both parents it would encourage the sharing of childcare responsibilities and the leave taken by any single employee would be unlikely to be excessive.

Access to telephones

A very simple step that employers can take is to ensure that all employees have access to telephones if they are concerned about a sick child, and to receive calls. It is equally important that parents can respond to urgent calls and leave to attend to a sick child if needed. Some parents reported that although they could, in principle, receive phone calls, their managers would disapprove of them being contacted at work. This creates additional and unnecessary stress.

Alternative arrangements for the care of sick children

Although paid leave to care for a sick child should be available, it must be recognized that many employers are reluctant or unable to drop everything to cope with this situation. A number of alternative policies which have been implemented by pioneering American organizations to help parents cope with a sick child without taking time off work have been found to be cost effective.[23] They include the following:

▌ in-home sick child care service – trained nurses or caregivers are sent to the child's own home when he/she is too ill to attend a nursery, or if the regular caregiver is ill.

▌ Mildly ill children may be cared for in a special room or wing of a workplace crèche, or in a hospital wing.

In Berkeley, California, a satellite sick child care programme has been set up, called 'Wheezles and Sneezles'.
This is located adjacent to a childcare centre and is staffed
by the same caregivers, so that they are familiar to the
children. It is visited by healthy children, so that if and
when they have to use it, it is not a strange environment.

Parents who take time off for domestic crises report feeling
guilty about letting down clients or customers. A 'locum' or
'supply' system of temporary staff to cover their absences
would reduce this pressure.

After-school programmes

Childcare problems do not disappear once a child begins
school. In some ways the situation becomes more difficult
as the length of the school day is shorter than the working
day. Employers can assist by arranging to transport children
from schools to their parents' workplace and many
companies also provide after-school childcare programmes.
School holidays can also present a problem for children too
old to attend a nursery but too young to be left at home
alone. Organizations or groups of organizations could assist
by offering holiday childcare or summer groups for employees' children. These are exempt from tax.

Perhaps more fundamentally, it is important that parents
are given the opportunity to take their vacation to coincide
with school holidays. Flexible working arrangements can be
used to enable parents to work longer in term time and save
up time to allow them a longer break during school holidays.
Term-time working contracts are also becoming increasingly
popular.

Parenting seminars

Parent education can – and should – be taken seriously by organizations. Some employers sponsor workshops at the workplace to address parenting issues ranging from the balancing of care of young children with a career, to dealing with schools or recognizing substance abuse in teenagers. As with all the initiatives described in this section, these seminars should be available for both mothers and fathers. At Midland Bank a working parents' network was launched officially by the Chief Executive in 1994 and has been meeting monthly in London, during lunchtimes, since 1992. The membership is approximately 75 per cent women, 25 per cent men. It offers a forum to share experiences and solutions to everyday problems faced by working parents and offers various support programmes, including parenting workshops, advice lines and literature. The aim is to extend this by establishing regional networks

Care of Elderly Parents and Other Relatives

We are living in an ageing society. The European Commission has predicted that by the end of this century one in four people in most member states will be over the age of 60. Nevertheless the issue of eldercare, the care of elderly or sick relatives, has received less attention than childcare to date. Traditionally care has been provided in the community by daughters or daughters-in-law who, having completed their childcare responsibilities, move on to the next phase of caring. This assumes no employment role for these women. The growing need for eldercare presents potentially a huge problem for dual-earner couples and their employers in this country. Without adequate public or corporate support, it is generally women's careers which are interrupted or curtailed. Many of the women and also some of the men we interviewed were aware of this as a potential future problem, or experienced guilt and conflict similar to that experienced by some mothers of young children as they attempted to balance paid work and caring responsibilities for elderly or sick parents.

Assistance with Eldercare

Much of what has been said about the problems of caring for young children also applies to employees who have responsibilities for elderly parents or for other sick or disabled relatives. Organizations genuinely committed to accommodating the link between work and family need to take these responsibilities into account. Many of the provisions for eldercare made by caring companies are based on and developed from those already in place for childcare, rather than developed specifically for this purpose – for example, family leave and information and retrieval services.[24] Other recently developed provisions in some large companies include counselling and referral services, eldercare guides or booklets, financial assistance, family leave and extended leave.[25] Some of the best eldercare schemes exist in paternalistic companies as an extension of their policies for their retirees. For example, Pilkington Glass has an extensive scheme funded by a charitable trust set up by the founding family. The service includes respite care, home visits, meals on wheels and other welfare services.

6 Looking at Alternatives

The workaholic syndrome demanded by many firms seriously diminishes personal and domestic life. An egalitarian dual-career relationship is unlikely to be a realistic goal for men working under this sort of pressure, while women often feel that they are forced to choose between career success and a family:

> If I want to get on, I have to be seen to be in the office from eight in the morning until eight at night. I am ambitious, but at some stage I would like to have children. Eventually I am just going to have to make difficult choices. (financial adviser, female)

Apart from the adverse personal effects of excessive work input, several of the participants in our research questioned the value of long hours in terms of productivity and efficiency. Some managers are aware of this:[1]

> We encourage people to work too long. They say it didn't do Fred any harm... The reality is that by encouraging people to work long hours you reward inefficiency.

> If people can't do it in a normal day they are either under-resourced, they are inefficient or they can't delegate properly and manage their time.

Many people work long hours, not because it is necessary from the point of view of productivity but in order to compete with their peers. Total involvement in work to the exclusion of all other aspects of life, together with competitiveness and the inevitable hostility which often creeps into this setting, may sound familiar. What is being described closely resembles the Type A stress-prone behaviour pattern (see Chapter 2). Such behaviour should be actively discouraged for the sake of the health of the workforce. Furthermore, competitive behaviour at work can cause job dissatisfaction, and may lower overall productivity.[2]

Organizations need to ask themselves the following questions:

1 Do employees need to work more than a 35-hour week? If so, why? At the turn of the century a 60-hour week was the norm. Perhaps we should now be re-evaluating the desirability of a 35-hour plus week.

2 What is the impact of excessive working hours on employees' family life?

3 What is the impact on employees' personal health?

4 Does the organization really benefit in the long term from long working hours?

Alternative Working Arrangements

There is a range of flexible working arrangements which can be introduced to increase employees' control over the hours they work, which would be of benefit to the dual-earner couple. When people are able to choose their working styles, they will be less stressed and, therefore, able to concentrate and perform better during the hours they work, with less worry about what is going on at home. Rigid, inflexible working hours are particularly stressful and inappropriate for parents of young children but, in fact, we found that most of the participants in our research, whether or not they had children, wanted more flexibility in their working lives.

Flexitime

Flexitime is a system which permits variable times of arrival and departure within the limits set by management. A standard number of hours have to be fulfilled during a given time, but the exact time can be flexible. Usually, but not always, there is a core period during which everyone must be in the office/building. This system does not create more time for family and home life, but it does provide you with more control over your life, enabling you to balance demands.

It can be extremely effective, therefore, in reducing the stress of combining work and family; it enables you to co-ordinate your working hours with the schedules of schools and nurseries, medical appointments, shopping and other obligations, and can help you avoid rush-hour traffic problems. However, to regard flexitime as useful only for working parents is to marginalize its importance. Flexitime has benefits for all employees, including those with a more conventional family set-up where the woman is assumed to be responsible for childcare and domestic matters.

The benefits of flexitime vary with the exact system used. Sheila Kamerman and Alfred Khan describe four different types of flexitime operating in the USA, from the least to the most flexible.[4]

- _Flexitour._ Employees choose their starting and ending times but must keep within the schedule they select and work the same number of hours each day.

- _Gliding time._ This is similar to flexitour, except that employees may vary the time they start and finish each day.

▌ *Variable day.* Employees can vary the number of hours worked each day, providing they are present for a minimum core period.

▌ *Maxiflex.* Daily hours can be varied as desired. Employees are not required to be present for any core period.

Systems allowing maximum flexibility enable employees to opt for innovative arrangements such as working a compressed working week. This involves working for ten or more hours a day for three or four working days. One choice could be an extended weekend which would benefit commuting couples. It can also be used by both parents of young children to enable them to manage childcare between them.

In 1995, 9.5 per cent of men and 14.7 per cent of women working full-time in Britain had flexitime. The second most popular form of flexibility was annualized hours, enjoyed by 6 per cent of full-time workers.[5] Within this system, employees' net working hours are decided for a whole year and then individuals are free to choose their own working times in order to fulfil the yearly quota.

This has advantages for both the employee and the organization. The employee is provided with the flexibility to work longer hours at certain periods and reduce working during periods such as school holidays, while retaining a secure and regular system of payment. Payment is by means of a regular monthly salary, regardless of the number of hours worked during that period. The benefits to employers will obviously depend upon the nature of the organization, but they may include improved ability to handle seasonal or cyclical fluctuations because of a more flexible workforce. The firm will be able to take full advantage of a vast pool of full-time, part-time, job sharing and even seasonal staff. Employees have the opportunity to work less than 40 hours a week without losing their full-time status, while temporary

Flexible working can also be arranged around shift work. For example, ASDA stores have recently introduced a number of new flexible working schemes to add to their existing programme:

▌ *Child care leave.* Parents can stop work for a short period, for example during school holidays, or choose to work shorter hours, or to work evenings and weekends for specific periods. They can return later with continuous service and maintained benefits. They can return to similar hours and a similar job.

▌ *Shift swapping schemes.* If parents or others need to be absent from work for specific domestic reasons, eg to take a child for hospital appointments, they can swap their shifts with colleagues without needing permission from management. They may, for example, be unable to work for two Wednesday afternoons. They can ask immediate colleagues to swap, or they may put up a notice on the staff notice board so that staff from other departments may swap. Asda argues that this meets everybody's needs. Staff do not have to lose pay and departments do not have to struggle because someone is away.

▌ *Study leave.* This scheme enables staff who undertake full-time study to return to work in the vacations or to work at weekends in term time and full-time in the vacation. Attempts are made to match up members of staff as a form of job share to benefit stores and their staff.

▌ *Store swapping schemes.* Employees who take up study away from their home may transfer to another store for short periods.

or seasonal staff enjoy a status change by becoming permanent employees. Finally, by fitting working time to people's needs, there is greater productivity and lower absenteeism and turnover.[6]

Companies which have not yet implemented a flexitime system should consider doing so. Others can review the adequacy of their system in the light of the needs of employees and of the organization. Employees' needs should be assessed, possibly through a company-wide survey, to determine which system would be most valuable. Once implemented, flexible working arrangements should be monitored to ensure that they are fulfilling needs and are available to the whole workforce. One woman we interviewed noted that the flexitime system operated by her organization was irrelevant to her as she was expected to be at work during the same hours as her boss. It is essential that flexitime is introduced as a means of providing employees with genuine *control* over the hours they work, and not as a token gesture.

Flexiplace

Helpful companies can be flexible about where, as well as when, employees work. Employees may be able to work at home or spread their workload between home and the office or workplace. Many different types of work are amenable to flexiplace, including editing, accounting, designing and computer programming. The limits to flexible locations are set by the need for contact with clients, patients or others and the need for specific equipment which is only available at the workplace. In some cases, clients may even be prepared to visit a person's home rather than a central workplace. There are obviously some situations in which the transfer of equipment, such as laboratory, to the home is not practical. Nevertheless, with the technological revolution an increasing amount of equipment can be used in alternative locations. The use of information technology, including personal computers, databases and fax systems, makes telecommuting, or teleworking, whereby employees work off-site, linked to a central office by a computer, increasingly feasible.

The growth of telecommuting has been partly in response to the need to retain the skills and expertise of experienced staff, especially women who have taken maternity leave. Working from home is not a solution to childcare, substitute childcare is still necessary. Nevertheless it can help employees with family responsibilities to achieve more flexibility to fit in work and childcare or other care. It is also of benefit to partners who work in different locations and is a possible solution to relocation problems. For instance, Jane, an area sales manager for a computer company in the South of England, is able to spend at least two or three working days a week telecommuting and staying in her home in the North, where her husband is based as a recruitment consultant.

ICL offer opportunities for off-site employment for trained computer personnel, who cannot or do not wish to undertake conventional full-time employment. In 1990, there were approximately 350 off-site employees. Hours are flexible, but employees contract to be available for a specified minimum number. Remuneration is at an hourly rate, calculated from the appropriate full-time annual salary. Off-site workers are graded, appraised and reviewed on the same terms as on-site staff, and are entitled to the same benefits, on a pro-rata basis. If you have family commitments this enables you to continue in interesting, worthwhile employment, and to return to full-time employment at a later date without having lost touch with the rapidly developing computer industry.

The instigation of homeworking involves investment in home computers and other equipment, but can be cost-effective in the long term. Apart from saving the expense of training new staff, the spread of telecommuting will ultimately reduce investment in office space and increase efficiency by reducing commuting time. It may also have a positive impact on pollution and the environment. However, homeworkers may feel isolated and cease to see themselves as members of the larger organization.[7] This effect can be reduced by providing homeworkers with at least a shared desk or office space for occasional office-based work and by regular meetings, and possibly by the arrangement of social events. Some managers persist in believing that they cannot trust people whom they cannot see. Often they fear losing control and power because of the lack of visible employees. The solution lies in education and training, whereby managers will realize that they will be able to supervise more people more efficiently, while at the same time responding to employees' family needs.[8]

Teleworking and the Family

Having an office at home can be very convenient and provide flexibility. However, it can also encroach upon the family. This may be either positive, for example, in helping children to learn about the world of work, or negative, for example if this limits space available to other family members or if the family is prevented from using the telephone or having friends to visit.[9] Here are some suggestions for teleworkers to ensure that the positives outweigh the negatives:

- Try to arrange a separate space for an office. This can then be clearly demarcated as your working area. Other family members will not be expected to intrude, but your work will not spill over to the rest of the house.

- A separate telephone line is also essential so that other family members are not restricted in telephone use.

- Self-discipline is essential. Teleworking provides the flexibility to integrate work and caring. However, the presence of an office in the home can also be a temptation for some workers to work all the time. It is important to make strict boundaries between work and family time.

- When there are young children in the home, childcare will still be necessary.

▌ It is important to have the support of other family
  members for teleworking.

▌ Isolation can be a problem so it may help to join a
  teleworkers club to meet for support and social reasons.

▌ It is necessary to be assertive with non-work-related
  callers during the day. Often friends and others will
  assume that if you are at home you are available.

▌ Women teleworkers are often sucked into combining
  work with traditional domestic roles, while some male
  teleworkers despite being home-based, shut themselves
  away and decline to have any involvement in domestic
  or childcare tasks. It is as important for teleworkers to
  confront issues of equality and sharing as it is for other
  workers.

Reducing Working Hours

Part-time Work

Part-time working often tends to be limited to relatively low-
status jobs, with restricted benefits and access to training
and opportunities for promotion. Organizations now need
to question the taken-for-granted assumption that only
employees who work full-time are serious about their
careers. When both spouses are employed, one or both can
afford to work part-time hours when their children are
young or while they have other family commitments.
However, highly trained individuals are unlikely to be
satisfied in dead-end jobs in which their skills are under-
utilized. What is needed are part-time jobs with career
opportunities, which take account of employees' family and
professional needs.

Job Sharing

If attendance on a full-time basis is essential, companies can consider offering job-share opportunities. The popularity of job sharing is growing for positions in management and elsewhere, in local authorities, banks, retail chain stores, firms of solicitors and a number of other types of organizations. Employers see the advantages in terms of retaining skilled and experienced staff. It is also recognized that working part-time allows people to stay fresh, energetic and creative during the hours worked, and there is evidence of greater productivity among job sharers.[10]

V-time

V-time or voluntary reduced time is a system which allows full-time employees to reduce working hours for a specified period, with a concomitant reduction in salary (see for example Lilly Industries). It differs from the usual concept of part-time work in that it is temporary, with a guaranteed opportunity to return to full time employment. Usually the schedule remains in force for a designated period, perhaps six or 12 months, to allow employees and employers to try the new arrangement, with the assurance that the commitment can be renegotiated or terminated after this period. All employee benefits are maintained during the period of reduced work, although they may be on a regular basis, such as shorter days or weeks, or may be a block of time, perhaps taken during school holidays. V-time is another useful strategy to create opportunities to balance work with other responsibilities, and may also be used by employees for gaining new skills or responding to a health problem.

Sabbaticals

Such opportunities can also be created by the use of sabbaticals, which are increasingly offered by large and small companies alike to employees with a certain level of service. Arrangements are usually made to cover absences by creating an opportunity for a trainee, or reorganizing colleagues' responsibilities to share out the work. This provides other employees with the opportunities to take on a higher level of responsibility which can contribute to personal and career development. Sabbaticals may be used for the care of sick relatives, for studying or people might wish to spend the time visiting adult children living abroad.

Easing the Transition to Parenthood or to Other Forms of Care

In Chapter 4, we discussed the problems associated with the transition to parenthood for dual-career couples. Similar transitions may occur if a close relative suffers a stroke or other crisis involving the need for sustained care. There are a number of innovative ways in which responsive organizations can, and do, help to ease the way for new parents or carers. The alternative work schedules discussed previously, particularly some form of reduced hours or phased return to work, are often welcomed during a period of transition. Some firms offer other benefits and concessions above the statutory minimum, for new parents. These include extended leave or financial benefits beyond the statutory maternity allowance. At the very least, organizations should ease the financial burden of maternity leave by covering job related items, such as membership fees for professional bodies and car expenses.

Network groups

These exist in several companies. They comprise women who have experienced maternity leave, who offer advice and support for those away from work and also for returners.

Workshops and seminars held during the firm's time, or in the lunch hour, can help new parents deal with issues ranging from feelings of guilt to childcare problems. As women returning from leave sometimes take a while to settle back into their routine, refresher courses can help them to reintegrate more easily. Above all, however, women value evidence that promotional decisions are made without regard to their family obligations.

Women who are self-employed, such as principals in medical practice or partners in firms of accountants, solicitors or architects, are not covered by legislation, and are therefore expected to make their own provision for maternity leave. A maternity clause could be automatically included in partnership deeds, so that women are not put in the position of having to raise and negotiate the issue at a time when they might feel it would prejudice their chances of admission to the partnership.

The question of time off for fathers for childcare has not yet emerged as a pressing issue for most men in the UK. Women are still widely perceived as being the primary parent. Nevertheless, we have seen that there are a growing number of fathers in dual-career relationships who would welcome the opportunity to be more involved in childcare. Paternity leave in various forms does exist in some organizations, although it is usually very brief and not always paid. Other men still suffer penalties, such as employer hostility, loss of pay or, in the extreme, job loss, if they take time off work around the time of childbirth. Better provisions for paid paternity leave would be of potential benefit to women and men, and to children, who would be able to form a closer bond with both parents. Parental leave, which is discussed in Chapter 8, is another way of enabling both parents to be involved in childcare while retaining continuity in their careers.

Career Break Schemes

Maternity and paternity leave will not be sufficient leave for all parents, some prefer to spend more time with their infants. Realizing that breaks for childcare are usually temporary, some organizations have taken steps to accommodate a longer career break. Re-entry and retainer schemes have been initiated to allow certain employees to interrupt their usual working arrangements for a number of years, after which they can return to the organization with no loss of seniority. The employee is usually expected to undertake at least two weeks' paid relief work for the organization during each year of her absence and is provided with regular information packs as well as a refresher course on her return. In practice many participants work for more than two weeks a year during their career break. The scheme may permit one five-year break or two shorter breaks, each commencing from the end of statutory maternity leave. Many women prefer two shorter breaks which enable them to return to work between the births of their children. Ideally, the choice of one long or two short breaks could be left to the employee. Career breaks are open, in principle, to both men and women, although in practice they tend to be taken exclusively by women. Organizations permitting two short career breaks could encourage the sharing of these between the two parents.

The benefits of operating a career break scheme are becoming increasingly apparent. For example:

▍ They ensure that participants remain in touch with their work, maintaining confidence and expertise.

▍ Firms operating these schemes will attract young women with talent and ambition, because of the reduced prospect of having to choose between family and career.

█ They ensure investment in training is not lost.

█ They enable successful employment at a future date with a minimum of retraining.

█ They provide role models of women successfully combining career and family.

█ They improve motivation, timekeeping and productivity.

█ They increase organizational flexibility by providing a pool of trained staff to draw on when people are absent or during peak periods.

█ They avoid skill shortages, especially in industries where it is difficult to attract female employees.

█ They reduce stress among new parents.

█ They reduce costs incurred in advertisements and reinstatement due to loss of continuity of staff.

Nevertheless some companies are now having to cut back on career breaks because of the difficulties in predicting the staff base five years ahead. From the employees' perspectives there may also be disadvantages. There is usually a condition that they may not take a job with another company during the period of leave. However, in unforeseen circumstances, such as the father being made redundant, this can create financial hardship, as career breaks are unpaid.[11] There is also no research yet assessing the impact of career breaks on employees' careers. However, they do add to the range of options available in many organizations, and increased choice increases parents' feelings of control (see Case Studies).

Assessing the needs of the workforce

The obvious benefits of certain alternative work patterns to organizations should not obscure the very specific needs of individuals or groups of employees. It is important for organizations to consult with the workforce to see what they consider most helpful. One national firm of chartered accountants, for example, surveyed staff to determine the potential demand for career breaks. Responses indicated very little demand for such schemes. Rather, professional staff favoured part-time or flexible work, to enable them to retain some involvement in work. Support staff also wanted to continue working, and felt that some form of childcare provision would be most helpful.

Finally, we would like to reiterate that both sexes have domestic responsibilities and thus, both men and women can benefit from policies which aim to ease the transition to parenthood and the management of work and family roles. Just as women need role models successfully combining career and motherhood, men require role models of fathers willing to accommodate their career for childcare. Organizations can play a part in bringing about the necessary change in attitudes by encouraging dual-career fathers who show an interest in paternity leave or career breaks, by sanctioning their choice and guaranteeing no damage to long-term career prospects. Ultimately, the most helpful organizations will be those offering the widest choice and flexibility to new parents to manage career and parenthood, in the way which suits their own individual needs.

Oxfordshire County Council

Oxfordshire has a range of flexible and family friendly options and a culture of accommodating employees' work–family needs.

The range of services provided by the County Council represents a number of different working time demands, including: 24 hour services with shift systems (eg fire services, social workers 'on call'); schools and other academic services based around the academic day/term/year; services influenced by increasing consumer demands eg libraries; and traditional office hours.

Within this context 57 per cent of all employees, and 67 per cent of women employees are employed part-time. Part-time work is not restricted to lower paid jobs. Eleven per cent of women on the two most senior management grades are part time. There are also a number of men working in part-time or job share posts.

The Council has a long history of developing flexible working options. Formal policies exist for:

- flexitime

- job sharing

- reduced hours

- career breaks and

- flexiplace (working from home).

Employees can also apply for up to one year's unpaid leave.

The Council report that a feature of their approach is its avoidance of complicated schemes and rule books, and its endorsement of a culture which encourages innovation, creativity and negotiation rather than tradition as the basis for determining employees' working arrangements. Not all options are available to all staff because of the particular demands of the services they work in. However, the aim is to make as many options as possible available to as many people as possible.

Other policies for reconciling work and family are:

▪ extended maternity leave

▪ paternity leave

▪ a number of workplace nurseries

▪ a summer holiday play scheme for school-aged children of employees.

The council emphasizes that these provisions are not just for women and not just for people with children, but believes all employees can benefit from a heathy balance between work and other areas of their lives.

It publishes a booklet on support for working carers, for those employees who care for elderly or sick relatives. This provides details of the various flexible working schemes which can support working carers, as well as compassionate leave (up to ten days a year paid leave to care for a sick relative) and details of where carers can receive confidential help, support and advice.

7 Training and Development

In this chapter we discuss training and development, which can contribute towards meeting the needs of the contemporary workforce at three levels:

- Management training to raise awareness of dual career family issues.

- Training which anticipates work and family issues.

- Training in skills which help employees to manage current work and family commitments.

We look at each type of training, and also provide some exercises which may be used as part of training or self-development programmes.

Management Training

Many managers are only too aware of dual-earner family dilemmas, having struggled with these themselves. Too often, however, senior management is made up primarily of men, the majority of whom have had non-career-orientated wives to shield them from family involvement. Consequently, companies such as Johnson and Johnson and IBM have introduced training programmes to encourage managers to become more sensitive to work and family issues. These programmes, which may be part of Managing Diversity training,[1] emphasize the business case for flexibility and reviewing corporate policy and practice in the light of workforce needs.

Management training can take the form of workshops or seminars, in which case studies of dual-earner family issues, such as those described in earlier chapters of this book, are considered. Open discussion of the specific needs of dual-earner spouses and single parents will help to overcome any taboo against discussing domestic commitments. An important function of such exercises must be the exploration of organizational culture and personal prejudices. Executives can be encouraged to clarify their own values about the ideal employee, career or parent, and if not to change them, then at least to value diversity, and consider how they can support the careers and lifestyles of all members of their company. It is also important for senior management to consider the example they set as role models. Evidence suggests that healthy executives value their family time.[2] Those who adopt a workaholic style should therefore consider the impact of this on themselves and also on newer members of their staff. It is important in this context to acknowledge that productivity is not just a function of the number of hours worked.[3]

It may be necessary as part of management training and awareness raising to explore reasons for the reluctance of some managers to consider family needs as relevant to a work context. This type of discussion can raise some painful issues. For example, some managers will have achieved career success by maximizing work involvement and sacrificing other aspects of their lives. Not infrequently this leads to marital conflict, divorce and/or difficult relationships with adolescent and adult children. Putting work–family issues on the agenda can thus face resistance.

Management training is important for senior managers and those who have power to implement change. It is also essential for supervisors and first-line managers to be trained to be adaptable and responsive, as they are key figures in determining the success of formal work–family policies.

Manager and supervisor training can be reinforced by a social auditing process which helps them look at the needs of employees with family commitments and the extent to which workplace policies and practices meet these needs and hence the needs of the organization. An example of this process is an audit of company policies and practices with respect to employees who are dual-earner parents of disabled children, but which could apply equally well to those with other childcare or caring responsibilities. An audit framework is currently being piloted at three organizations, one each in the private, public and voluntary sectors.[4]

The audit framework is presented as a list of discussion questions which can be used in focus groups as part of management training in work and family issues. Managers consider the business case for change. They then discuss what they know about their workforce in terms of work and family needs, and look at their policies and practices, and aspects of organizational culture, as well as considering how they can work with the community to ensure the necessary childcare and other support are available to their workers. In each case they discuss not only the present situation but also what it would take to introduce changes towards greater flexibility and support.

Training Which Anticipates Work–Family Issues

Training can encourage people to consider work–family issues before they arise. This may be accomplished within courses in personal effectiveness and career or life planning. The aim of these courses is to enable employees at an early stage in their career to consider their short- and long-term goals, to identify their strengths and resources towards achieving these ends, and also to identify the possible barriers and consider ways of overcoming these. It is increasingly acknowledged that for women this process must involve a consideration of present and future family plans which are intimately bound up with career issues. The issues arising from earlier chapters suggest that men as well as women need to consider career goals in the context of broader life goals.

Personal effectiveness training usually takes place in small, participative groups to facilitate a sharing of ideas and exploration of issues within a supportive context. The issues which arise often include, for example:

| if and when to have children

| possible impact on careers

| location and mobility issues

| what happens if one person's career takes off and not the partner's

| unequal sharing of domestic work and

| sex discrimination at work.

Discussion can focus on identifying strategies for overcoming barriers. The value of open discussion of these issues is that:

1   People realize that they are not alone in facing decisions and obstacles, and hence the personal becomes political.

2   Anticipation of problems in advance gives participants the opportunity to plan and take control of their

lives. Individuals or couples can explore their own flexible way of managing their lives together rather than responding to societal norms or company expectations.

3   Various choices can be discussed and new and creative ideas explored such as commuter marriage (see Chapter 3) or role cycling. Role cycling[5] is a type of career and life planning used by some dual-career couples to ensure that intense work and family demands do not occur simultaneously, and that the maximum demands on each partner do not overlap. For instance, one partner may delay a particular activity such as studying for a further degree or seeking a promotion, until later in the family cycle when childcare demands or the spouse's work demands have diminished. Each partner will have the opportunity to do these things with the support of their partner, but at different stages. This approach involves long-term planning and a willingness for both partners to be flexible and to accommodate the other. It may mean that opportunities cannot always be taken as and when they arise, and that certain ambitions may have to be deferred. On the positive side role cycling may be used to create opportunities for both partners at a time when it is convenient to them as a couple, avoiding overload on the way.

The following exercise might help an individual or couple to focus on work and family issues, now and in the future.

Exercise 1

Aim To help participants to start to focus on life and career development issues.

1 Draw a 'lifeline', using any visual form (a line, circle, etc). You may prefer to draw two lines, for life and career, with intersections as relevant.

2 Mark where you are now. Indicate the most personally significant events in your life or career to date.

3 Indicate what you expect to be doing in the next x years (up to whatever age you choose). Indicate what you expect to be the significant events in the future, and when you would like them to occur.

4 Share these lifelines in pairs and perhaps in groups of four and discuss the implications.

Skills for Managing Work and Family Commitments

The objectives of work–family management training is to help you reflect on actual and/or anticipated work–family issues and to identify and develop strategies for managing dual roles. There are three main components of such a programme:

▮ managing work–family conflict and overload

▮ assertiveness skills for work–family management and

▮ stress management.

Managing Conflict and Overload

Coping with conflict

Psychologists have identified three general approaches to coping with role conflict:[6]

▎ _Type 1 coping: changing other people's expectations._ This is an attempt to alter other people's expectations of a particular role. For instance, a wife may renegotiate with her husband the expectation that she should be responsible for all domestic work, or an employee may negotiate with his or her boss about what should be expected in a particular job. Type 1 strategies include delegation and refusing to take on extra work (by being assertive).

▎ _Type 2 coping: changing self-expectations._ This is an attempt by an individual to change his or her own self-expectations and behaviours without necessarily trying to alter other people's attitudes. Making a personal decision to limit activities in the career, spouse or parental roles would be examples of Type 2 coping. Strategies include eliminating roles, for example, giving up voluntary work or union activity, restricting social contacts and establishing priorities.

▎ _Type 3 coping: role expansion 'pleasing everyone'._ Instead of attempting to change the situation or alter self-expectations, an individual may attempt to organize himself or herself in such a way that all role demands can be met. For instance, an overworked mother may work even harder to fit the superwoman image rather than delegating more domestic work to other family members, reducing work involvement, or lowering standards in the home. Strategies which enable individuals to do all this include planning, scheduling, working harder and denying that a situation is stressful.

Types 1 and 2 coping are both active coping strategies: they involve an attempt to change the situation in order to make it more manageable. Type 3 coping is more passive. It involves an acceptance of all demands made. Attempts are made to satisfy everyone's expectations by being more organized or by using techniques which will minimize the subsequent stress without eliminating or reducing its cause.

Exercise 2

Aim To begin to identify your own approaches to coping with work–family conflict and to consider alternatives.

1 Draw a diagram depicting yourself (in any form, eg a circle or other symbol) and the people or institutions which make demands on your time. (For example, you might draw yourself as a circle and various other circles around you, representing partner, children, parents, manager, colleagues etc.)

2 Identify the demands which are self-generated.

3 Identify which of these demands conflict with each other.

4 Discuss your diagram with a partner. Where do conflicting demands come from? Who or what are the greatest source of demands? To what extent are demands self-generated? What is the impact of social and organizational expectations?

Look at some of the conflicts identified in your diagram and

5 Consider the types of coping you generally use. Are they Type 1, 2 or 3?

What are the pay offs for the strategies? The costs?

Would other strategies have greater pay offs? Costs?

Research shows that role redefinition (changing our own or other people's expectations) tends to be more successful than role expansion strategies (see Table 2). These strategies produce higher levels of career satisfaction and have been found to be more successful than role expansion in reducing conflicts between work and home.[7] The redefinition of roles

Table 2 *Examples of role redefinition and role expansion strategies*

	Role redefinition	Role expansion
	Conflict Area	Conflict Area
	Taking child to mid-day dentist appointment when committee meeting is scheduled, only to wait and wait.	Being concerned over some work pressure and not having the time for caring for children's emotional concerns.
Side 1 (Professional)	'I've just been appointed to the committee. We are to make important decisions for the rest of the year.'	'I need to have evidence of success, and fast.'
Side 2 (Maternal)	'Child needs a filling for the first time and is frightened. We have discussed it but she's still scared.'	'The children need me as a caring, listening supporter.'
Other Information	New job. Had not asked spouse to do medical or dental visits before.	
Solution	Talked with spouse and he took child to dentist, making up the time he took off at the weekend.	It keeps happening, I just keep going.

Source: Lucia A. Gilbert, Carole K. Holohan and Linda Manning, *Coping with Conflict Between Professional and Maternal Roles*[9]

is particularly effective in dealing with work-related problems and with issues concerning relationships between partners but diehard attitudes towards motherhood often make it very difficult, even for 'non-traditional' women, to alter their own or other people's expectations of what makes a good mother.[8]

Recognizing overload

Before steps can be taken to redefine expectations to reduce pressures it is necessary to recognize that a problem exists. Overload, in particular, is often accepted as a fact of life and not defined as a problem. An interesting study of 164 professional women conducted by Sarah Yogev in the USA revealed that mothers of young children worked a total of 107 hours a week or more in fulfilling their professional and parental duties.[10] Yet these women did not report feeling more overworked than childless women whose total hours were much shorter. This can be explained in terms of women's socialization experiences. Most contemporary professional women were socialized initially into traditional attitudes towards the roles of wife and mother and may, therefore, evaluate their performance in family roles by comparing themselves with housewives. However, they have also been socialized into their professional roles, and evaluate their professional competence by comparing themselves with male colleagues. Subsequently, women take it for granted that having chosen to combine professional and family roles they will have little time for themselves. Admitting to being overburdened appears to be an admission of inadequacy, implying that they are unable to integrate the two areas of their lives. For men, admitting that hours of work are too long or that the pressure is too great, can also appear to be a sign of weakness due to their early conditioning, professional socialization and the internalization of the male work ethic.

Exercise 3

Are you suffering from overload?

Consider whether any of the following statements apply to you. If so, it may be that you are suffering from overload and should consider steps to reduce your workload or to cope better with this situation.

I feel as though I am constantly under pressure.

I am constantly tired.

I feel that I have too much work to do in the time available.

I find my work too difficult and have difficulty coping with it.

There do not seem to be enough hours in the day to get everything done.

Exercise 4

To be completed prior to a course, or after a course, to reinforce the message.

Keep a diary for a typical week, noting how many hours are spent:

a) in work-related activities

b) in domestic work

c) in childcare

d) travelling.

Add up your total hours for the week. If they are excessive and you have agreed with any of the statements in Exercise 3, ask yourself whether your combined workload really is inevitable?

Once it is recognized that the overload and conflict inherent in the dual-earner lifestyle are a consequence of conflicting expectations and not personal inadequacy, it should be possible to examine the sources of stress.

Dealing with overload

One way of managing multiple roles and avoiding overload and conflict, is to establish clear priorities, rather than attempting to excel at everything. If you are certain where your priorities lie you can decide which life goals to concentrate on, and which activities can be relinquished or at least given less attention.

Exercise 5

Aim Establishing priorities and goals
Below are a list of life goals. Assign a value to each one according to their priority in your life. Place a '1' in the column next to that area of your life which you value most, a '2' next to that which you value second and so on. This will help clarify where your priorities lie. Given that it is not practical to try to achieve everything at the same time, you can use this list to help you decide where to direct your energies. You may decide that the lowest priorities indicate that there are certain activities which you may have to reduce or even eliminate to enable you to achieve your major life goals.

Life Values	Priority
Work	
Children	
Marriage	
Other family relationships	
Service to others	

Friendships

Financial security

Achievement

Success

Creativity

Good health

Independence

Leisure activities

Other (Please specify)

Having clarified your priorities it may be useful to consider some strategies for reducing overload from work, family, or both.

Strategies for reducing overload

Questioning the need for long hours at work. If the family or other values are equal to or more important than your career, you may wish to question the need to put in long hours at work, to work overtime, or to bring work home in the evenings. The workaholic syndrome is encouraged or expected in many organizations. It is difficult to challenge a corporate work ethic. Nevertheless, clear priorities may lead to decisions to reduce your hours of work, at least for a short time, perhaps while the children are young or an elderly relative is sick.

Delegation. There are usually two obstacles to the use of this strategy: a belief that we must do everything ourselves because nobody else can do it as efficiently; and a reluctance to relinquish power and control. Even if we do believe, (perhaps justifiably) that nobody can perform our work as efficiently as we can, it is important to consider whether such a level of expertise is always necessary. If responsibilities are not delegated at some point, other people will not develop the requisite skills.

The second obstacle, reluctance to relinquish power and control, suggests a feeling of insecurity and excessive competitiveness typical of the Type A stress-prone person-ality (see Chapter 2). This type of attitude can itself contribute towards stress and illness and should be avoided. The importance of delegation applies to family work as well as occupational demands, and is often rejected for the same two reasons. Many women do not want to give up ultimate control over home and children, and men are loathe to give up the much greater power that goes with being the major breadwinner. As in the work situation, it is only by tolerating other people's initial ineptness that some of the domestic chores can eventually be delegated.

Lowering standards in the home: Challenging the superwoman myth! Overload can be reduced by altering the demands in non-work areas of life. Given the problems associated with childcare discussed in earlier chapters, a decision may be made to limit your family to one child, or not to have children at all. If this is considered too high a price to pay, lowering your domestic standards is a good strategy. Two partners with intense career involvement cannot compete with a full-time homemaker. Often full-time homemakers are perfectionists, but is it realistic to adopt such standards in addition to a full-time career? Below we consider some strategies for tackling the superwoman myth, based on work carried out in the US.[11]

▌ Do things effectively. This does not mean that they have to be done perfectly.

▌ Explore unrealistic beliefs. These may be 'I have to be perfect at everything I do' or 'I have to spend every minute when I am not working, with my children', and these create stress.

▌ Prioritize your domestic work and decide what compromises can be made.

▌ Ask yourself what will happen if you do not do everything perfectly. Are your fears realistic?

▌ Examine your guilt about childcare. Consider our discussion about the effects of working parents on children in Chapter 4. Is your guilt really justified?

Considering alternative ways of working. If family is a much greater priority than career or ambition, it may be useful to consider alternative ways of working (see Chapter 6), including not only those in place in your organization, but also other possibilities that you may actively campaign for, or might encourage policy-makers to consider. However, most strategies have both advantages and disadvantages and these should be considered in the light of individual needs and circumstances (see Table 3).

Job sharing may be particularly worthwhile considering, because many of the problems of part-time work are eliminated, as fringe benefits as well as salary are divided between the sharers. This option can be used to create opportunities in jobs and at levels which are not normally available on a part-time basis.

Table 3 *Some alternative work patterns – advantages and disadvantages for employees*

Strategy	Advantages	Disadvantages
Part-time work	Enables parents to spend more time with children. Enables new parents to keep in touch with their career while children are young. Reduces overload and conflict. Creates flexibility.	Reduces income and other benefits. May reduce opportunities for promotion. Not usually available in high-level jobs. Often undertaken by women in addition to domestic responsibility – so less equality in relationship.
Working from home	Creates flexibility. Cuts down on travelling time. Facilitates return from maternity leave for women. May reduce childcare problems or schedule incompatibility. May be used to solve relocation problems.	May be limited opportunities. Partner at home may take greater share of domestic responsibility. May be reduced opportunities for promotion. Lack of social interaction with colleagues.
Job sharing	Facilitates return from maternity leave for women. Reduces conflict between work and family. Reduces childcare problems. Creates flexibility. Could be available in a wide range of occupations at all levels. Fringe benefits are retained. *If both partners job share:* Increases equality and interdependence in relationship.	Reduced income (but not other benefits). Half a job tends to have more than half the workload. Difficulty in persuading some employers/colleagues to implement.

Husband and wife job-sharing social workers – Lynda and John

When Lynda and John were married they were both working as generic social workers. In 1982 they were involved in union activity and in the drawing up of a project for job sharing by the city council. This coincided with their wish to start a family. They began to job share shortly before their first child was born. They now have two children. John covered for Lynda and worked full-time during her two periods of maternity leave. After each leave, Lynda returned to share the job and they shared the childcare between them. In 1986 they successfully applied together for a new job as team leader. They each work for two or three days, on alternative weeks. Full consultation is provided for all team members at all times, but they split the staff for regular support and management. In order to ensure continuity they try to liaise with each other as much as possible often reading each other's files and discussing work a great deal at home. They also make sure that they both attend team meetings regardless of which half of the week they occur in. On the whole they believe that the team feel that they benefit from having two managers.

They both consider that job sharing has proved to be an ideal solution to the problems of combining career and family. According to John:

> It has enabled me to play a full part in bringing the children up. It is unusual for a man to have this opportunity and Lynda has had continuity in her career. We felt that it was important to look after the children ourselves while they were very young. We were able to do that. Overall it has worked well. Perhaps we do end up working more than half a week each to ensure a smooth transition, but it's a sacrifice that is well worthwhile.

Now that their children are a little older they are able to use job sharing for another purpose – Lynda is taking a further degree and John has once again taken over the job full-time to cover for her absence.

Assertiveness and Work–Family Management

We have seen that the most effective strategies for managing work–family conflict and overload involve an attempt to change other people's expectations. The strategies require effective communication and negotiation which are part of assertiveness skills. Assertiveness is the art of confident, clear, honest and direct communication, while at all times retaining respect for other people and is an essential skill for those managing work and family demands. It is useful in transactions with family members, employers, colleagues and others. The assertive person is open and flexible and genuinely concerned about the rights of others, yet at the same time is able to establish his or her own rights. These include:

▌ The right to make mistakes.

▌ The right to set your own priorities.

▌ The right for your own needs to be considered as important as the needs of other people.

▌ The right to refuse requests without feeling guilty.

▌ The right to express yourself as long as this does not violate the rights of others.

▌ The right to judge your own behaviour, thoughts and emotions and to take the responsibility for the consequences.

Assertive behaviour is non-defensive and non-manipulative. The assertive person can be distinguished from aggressive individuals who deny the rights of others and from passive individuals who deny their own rights (see Table 4).

Table 4 Examples of passive, aggressive and assertive responses to given situations

Situation	Responses		
	Passive	*Aggressive*	*Assertive*
Asking partner to do more housework while you are busy on a project.	I don't know how I am going to manage all the housework while I'm so busy. (This is indirect – not asking openly for help.)	You know I've got a lot on at the moment, and you never pull your weight in the house. (Blaming other person – not taking responsibility for own needs.)	I am very busy at the moment. Can we sit down and discuss how we could rearrange the housework. (Provides opportunity for discussion and gives reason.)
Asking to begin work half an hour later, because of nursery school hours.	It's really difficult for me to get to work for 9.00, but I'll try and make arrangements. (Hoping for concession – but not asking directly.)	There's no reason why I shouldn't be late for work sometimes. I do have family responsibilites, you know.	I am unable to be here before 9.30 because I have to drop my child at nursery at 9.00. Can we discuss how I can fit my work in? (Does not allow possibility of outright refusal – being reasonable, asking for a discussion.)
Refusing to do overtime/ take on extra work.	I'd really rather not, but I suppose if you can't get anybody else… (Does not accept own right to say 'no'.)	There must be other people you could ask. Why pick on me? (Does not accept other person's right to ask the question.)	No. I realize that you have a problem finding someone to do it, but I cannot do it at the moment. (Accepts other person's right to ask the question.)
A woman being asked at interview if she intends to have children.	I don't know. Maybe in a few years' time. (Accepts the question.)	You've no right to ask me that question. You wouldn't ask a man. (Defensive – albeit technically correct.)	I'm sorry I don't see the point of the question. What is it you are really asking? (Asks for clarification – tries to turn the question into a more direct, assertive question such as, How long will you be working for us?)

Assertive skills

Essential skills for assertive interaction include:

▍ Being able to decide what it is you want or feel and to say so specifically and directly.

▍ Sticking to your statement, repeating it if necessary, over and over again.

▍ Deflecting any manipulative response from the other person which might undermine your assertive stance.

▍ Active listening.

▍ The ability to reach a joint solution.

Be specific. This means deciding what the point you want to make is and stating it without the unnecessary padding which we often use when we are anxious or uncomfortable. Consider the statement below. The main point is italicized, the rest is padding.

> I know it's not good for people to take time off during the day, and I've never done it before but *I have to take my child to the doctors this afternoon.* He's got this awful rash and I'm quite worried about it.

Compare the impact of the specific statement, and the padded version. Padding tends to weaken the impact of a statement and confuse the listener.

Stick to your statement, repeating if necessary. This involves a technique known as 'broken record'. Basically it is the skill of calm repetition. By repeating what you want to say over and over again, it is possible to ignore manipulative side-tracking and irrelevancies. Here is an example:

Parent:	I don't feel that you are doing enough to help in the house. I would like you to put the washing in the machine in the mornings.
Teenage son:	I haven't got time to do that.
Parent:	I appreciate that you are rushed in the morning, but I would like you to put the washing in.
Son:	Other kids don't have to do that sort of thing.
Parent:	I know different families have different routines but I would like you to put the washing on in the mornings.
Son:	Well, it's not fair.
Parent:	I'm sorry you don't think it's fair, but I would like you to put the washing on in the morning.

Fielding responses. This is the ability to indicate you have heard what the other person has said without being sidetracked from your main purposes. It is illustrated by the responses of the parent in the above dialogue and also in the following example:

1st colleague:	Can you cover for me tonight?
2nd colleague:	No, I'm sorry, I can't work late tonight.
1st colleague:	But I've often covered for you in the past. I thought I could rely on you. (Attempt to manipulate by instilling guilt.)
2nd colleague:	Yes, I appreciate that you have covered for me in the past, (fielding) but I can't work late tonight.

Active listening. Assertive encounters are facilitated by active listening, that is, demonstrating that you have heard what the other person is saying. Sometimes this involves picking up emotions that may have been expressed through words or body language. For example, if you are being accused of not pulling your weight either at home or at work, rather than becoming defensive, which would exacerbate conflict, you can respond by saying, 'You seem very angry/disappointed'. This will help the other person to clarify what she or he feels and wants and you can then go on to discuss this constructively.

Negotiating a joint solution. If you present your point of view clearly and specifically, saying what exactly you want to happen, but also listen actively to what the other person is saying, it may become clear that there is a genuine gap between what you each want and need. You can then begin to work towards a joint solution, which is acceptable to both, that is, a win–win situation rather than a win–lose situation. In a win–lose situation one person feels put down and future conflict is guaranteed.

Using Assertive Skills to Deal with Work–Family Dilemmas

Assertive skills together with other work–family management skills can be applied in dealing with specific dilemmas, such as mobility, sexism and relationship problems.

Mobility – exploring possibilities and alternatives

It is often necessary for couples faced with the prospect of the relocation of one partner to deviate from accepted norms of behaviour. The traditional pattern is for the woman to move with the man's job, while the man moving with the woman's job is non-traditional. As we discussed in Chapter 3, there are various strategies between these two extremes. Making your position clear from the outset may be one way of anticipating and avoiding future dilemmas. There are a range of positions which can be stated clearly upon taking up employment:

▌ Make it clear that you will not be willing to relocate.

▌ Make it clear that you will not be willing to relocate unless a suitable position is also found for your partner.

▌ Make it clear from the outset that you are willing to relocate and that your family poses no obstacle. This may be particularly necessary for married women who may be passed over for promotion on the assumption that they cannot be mobile.

▌ State that requests for relocation will be considered in the light of circumstances at the time, including your partner's career situation, children's schooling and so on.

At a later stage, dilemmas may still arise. If so, there are a number of options, for example:

▌ Refuse to relocate. This may involve loss of promotion and will reflect your life priorities.

▌ If the new location is not too geographically distant, consider moving so that both of you can travel to work from one home which is approximately equidistant from your work locations. This may involve substantial travelling time.

▌ Consider alternating relocation decisions in each partner's favour. A move may be made now to facilitate one person's career on the understanding that the next move will favour the other's.

▌ Consider living apart during the week or for longer periods.

▌ Ask is it possible for one partner to work from home.

Any decision will involve some sacrifice, in terms of career prospects, family life or travelling time. Your final decision will depend upon where your priorities lie in terms of your life values.

Working towards more egalitarian relationships between men and women at home

With shortage of time and energy and uneasiness about changing gender expectations between dual-earner couples, resentment, anger and confusion can accumulate. It is important for partners to learn to communicate with each other and to be aware of each other's feelings.

Unless there is a clear, open contract delineating the roles and responsibilities of each partner, misunderstandings and conflicts may occur. Cary Cooper, Rachel Cooper and Lynn Eaker[12] suggest a strategy of semi-formalized family negotiation meetings in which all family members can be involved. This avoids conflicts and resentments by providing a clear action plan. They suggest a six-stage role renegotiation strategy:

Step 1.   Prepare a balance sheet of work and home commitments, listing details of hours spent and tasks undertaken.

Step 2.   Call a formal family meeting to share concerns and discuss the detailed balance sheet.

Step 3.   Renegotiate various family commitments.

Step 4.   Create mutual action plans for the next three months which are agreed by all family members.

Step 5.   Review success or otherwise of action plans at the end of a three-month period.

Step 6.   Develop new action plans based on experience of previous one. Continue the process until all parties are satisfied with the arrangements.

If tensions within a family have already reached a stage of conflict and hostility, lack of effective communication between partners may preclude the possibility of reneg-otiating roles. It is necessary to find a way of reducing hostilities and reopening channels of communication. Here are some steps that can be taken:

▌ *Find time to talk in a relaxed way.*   This may involve deliberately setting aside some time from busy schedules when lack of interruptions is guaranteed.

▌ *Use assertive techniques for effective communication.*   Using the wrong words can alienate. It is better to take respons-ibility for your own feelings and behaviour, than to accuse - eg to say 'I feel you could do more in the house' rather than 'you never do enough in the house'. Your feelings can be discussed but an accusation merely makes the other person defensive.

▌ *Listen to what the other person says.* It is useful to reflect back, to show that you have really heard and accept his or her feelings. For example, 'It sounds as though you feel really angry with me. Can you tell me what it is that I do which makes you feel that way?'

If problems have become really overwhelming:

▌ It might help to agree an official time out or call a temp-orary truce. A temporary separation, such as separate holidays, may provide time to work out a solution.

▌ Don't try to solve all problems at once. Work on one at a time.

▌ If necessary, elicit the help of a professional counsellor.

Countering sexism and discrimination at work

We saw in Chapter 3 that sexism and discrimination at work can exacerbate career issues for dual-career families. Knowing your rights is important in dealing with sexism and discrimination at work. If necessary the help of the Equal Opportunities Commission can be enlisted in fighting for these rights. However, the remedies are often financial settlements rather than restoration of career opportunities. It may be worthwhile considering how it might affect you as an individual before taking a stand. It is important for women to be prepared for the possibility of sexism and to anticipate how this can be dealt with. For instance if personal questions about marriage and family are asked at interviews, how should this be dealt with? Below are some suggestions:

▌ Point out that the question is discriminatory and refuse to answer. This is correct but might be interpreted as aggressive.

▌ Point out that the question is discriminatory, but be prepared to answer anyway in such a way as to assure the panel that there are no obstacles to you fulfilling all the duties required in the job.

▌ Ask why the question is considered relevant. This is the most assertive reply and should force the interviewer to ask a more direct question such as how long will you be working in this job? You can then point out that this depends on your success in the organization.

█ Use the question to lead to talking about your strengths. For instance you might say that you have always employed a nanny because you worked such long hours in your previous job; or your husband has had to accept that your devotion to work leaves no time for children; or other people have commented that managing a career and family will pose no problems for someone with your organizing skills.

The important point is not to be caught off-guard, but to be prepared for these questions, even though they should not arise.

Stress Management Training

While it may be possible to change our own ideas about the roles of men and women at home and at work, other people's attitudes may take a little longer to alter. Organizational expectations may also be resistant to change. In addition, there is always the possibility of short-term stress when the demands of work or family or both are particularly intense. It is useful to have ways of managing temporary or short-term stress as it arises.

The exercises below can be used for group or individual stress management training.

Time Management

When we asked dual-career spouses how they coped with their busy lifestyle their first reaction was usually to extol the virtues of good organization. Attempting to do too much in a short space of time can create pressure. The best technique for reducing this stress may be to cut down on some of the tasks to be performed but this is not always possible or desirable. The alternative is to use time-management techniques which involve the balancing of supply and demand. By working out how to balance your demands with the time you have available it is possible to schedule tasks into the most effective order and to avoid pressure.

Exercise 6

Aim   To draw up a balance sheet of time demands and supply

Time demands:

▍ List all tasks, both work and family, which need to be completed within a given time interval, such as for the following week.

▍ Estimate how much time each task will take.

▍ Increase the time estimates by 10–15 per cent to provide a margin of error for dealing with unexpected problems. If you set yourself too little time for each task, this will increase the pressure on you.

Time supply:

▍ For the week you are planning, identify the blocks of time available each day for completing necessary tasks. Deduct realistic times for travelling, eating, relaxing and so on.

▍ Match the tasks to be accomplished with the time blocks available so as to use the available time most constructively.

▍ If you find there is not enough time available, work out priorities. List tasks in order of importance. Make sure that the most important task will be completed and leave the least important to be tackled only if extra time becomes available. An imbalance of supply and demand makes it apparent that some of the other active strategies discussed earlier, such as delegation, must be considered. In determining the priority of tasks to be fitted into your busy time schedule, be aware of the importance of activities which reduce stress. Designating relaxation as a low priority may work on a very short-term basis, but will have adverse effects on your health in the long term as low priority tasks are rarely accomplished.

Recognizing and Modifying Stress-producing Behaviour

The impact of certain personality characteristics and behavioural styles which can increase stress has been mentioned in earlier chapters. Foremost among these is the Type A behaviour pattern. Type A individuals create stress for themselves at work by imposing constant deadlines, refusing to delegate, and by their competitiveness and aggressive personal style. Type A behaviour is particularly incompatible with the dual-career lifestyle as it usually leads to heavy workloads and a tendency to become so involved in work that other aspects of life are relatively neglected.[13] It increases the potential for interference between work and family. It may also spill over into the marital relationship causing dissatisfaction and conflict.[14] In our study, Type A behaviour was one of the major causes of stress for dual-earners.

Training Type A individuals to modify their behaviour encourages people to recognize the pattern in themselves and others, and then introduces ways of changing these responses. Several of the coping strategies discussed earlier, such as delegation, time management and developing assertiveness skills to enable people to say 'no' to additional work, are useful. In addition there are a number of exercises based on behaviour modification techniques which can be used. These include encouraging Type As to:

- set realistic goals about which aspects of their personality they can change and how long it might take;

- make a contract with themselves for each goal. Write it down and work on one modification at a time. Make these goals very specific, for instance, 'For two weeks I will not stamp my feet and fume when queuing';

- plan no more than they have time for;

▌ plan one event a week that puts friendship before work or encourages a sense of fun;

▌ rehearse situations which create anger or anxiety, and practise responding calmly;

▌ enlist help from family and friends in trying to change;

▌ find someone who is not Type A to serve as a role model;

▌ learn relaxation techniques to use under stress;

▌ look for subtle changes which show they are succeeding and reward themselves.

Cognitive Reappraisal – Perceiving the Situation as Non-stressful

An individual becomes stressed only if she or he appraises an event as stressful. It is stressful to feel helpless in the face of a potential threat, but the threat is reduced if an individual believes he or she can cope with the situation. This is why 'hardy' people remain healthy in the face of pressure.[15] They perceive their situation as meaningful, challenging and controllable.

There are a number of techniques which can be used to cognitively reappraise stressful situations. One such technique is to compare your own situation with alternatives, which might help to emphasize the advantages as well as the pressures in your chosen lifestyle. Margaret Paloma reported that the women in her study reduced tension by defining the dual-career pattern as favourable and advantageous in comparison with being a housewife.[16] Women who have spent a period of time at home looking after small children often use this technique. Men who recognize the advantages of a dual-career marriage, also compare themselves favourably with single breadwinners. However, other men compare themselves unfavourably with the husbands of housewives, because of the extra domestic input which is expected of them. The latter types are more likely to become depressed, because they define their situation in a negative way.[17] Comparing yourself unfavourably with other people creates stress. It is important to select a realistic reference group to illustrate your own advantages, to instill a sense of control and challenge, and to avoid feelings of disadvantage and self-pity.

A technique which can be used to alter the appraisal of specific stressful events is constructive self-talk (see Table 5). This refers to the words we say to ourselves when confronted with challenging situations. These range from constructive encouraging to harshly condemning, negative self-talk. Negative self-talk uses self-defeating words such as 'can't' and 'never'. It uses up emotional energy and achieves nothing, promoting stress. Constructive self-talk encourages a positive perception of the situations and reduces stress.

Exercise 7

Aim To practise the skill of constructive self-talk

Write down the things you say to yourself in stressful situations. If you are using self-defeating negative self-talk, try to work out the more constructive alternatives. These should be encouraging, but also realistic. You will not be convinced by something totally unrealistic, such as 'I'm going to give the most perfect performance imaginable' whereas a more modest, 'I'll take a deep breath and do my very best' is encouraging and realistic.

Table 5 *Examples of constructive and negative self-talk*

Situation	Negative Self-talk	Constructive Self-talk
Overload	I'll never get all this done.	There's a lot to do. I'll take one step at a time and it will be really satisfying when it is all finished.
After maternity leave	I'm so out of touch, I can't get back into the swing of things.	Everyone has some difficulty getting back to work. It'll take some effort, but I'll enjoy the challenge.
Marital conflict	Our marriage will never recover from this setback. He/she is impossible to live with.	We've been through a difficult patch but we can try and work it out.
Interview	I'm so nervous I can't think straight.	I'll take a deep breath and relax. Then I'll enjoy presenting myself in the best light.
Feelings of guilt	I shouldn't be working full time. I feel so guilty about leaving the baby. I'll always feel guilty.	There is no reason for me to feel guilty. The baby is in good hands at the nursery. Other children come to no harm and neither will mine.

Questioning irrational beliefs

Being realistic and rational in your beliefs is important in determining how you appraise situations. Irrational beliefs create stress. These include such beliefs as:

▌ I must be perfect at everything I do, otherwise I'm a failure.

▌ Everybody must admire me.

▌ I should be available to my child every minute of the day.

▌ If our marriage is to be a success we should never, ever argue.

Exercise 8

Aim   To question stress-producing irrational beliefs

We have already discussed irrational beliefs underlying the superwoman syndrome. Setting standards of personal behaviour which are impossible to achieve guarantees stress. Examine the 'musts' and 'shoulds' which govern your life, and ask yourself whether they are realistic and rational. If not, try to substitute more realistic expectations of yourself.

   Sometimes people become obsessed with negative self-talk, irrational beliefs, guilt or even rational anxiety. This problem can be effectively attacked through the techniques of thought-stopping and mental diversion. _Thought stopping_ involves visualizing, or even saying out loud, the word 'STOP', as soon as you become aware of self-defeating thoughts. It should then be possible to switch to a pleasant relaxing image, as a diversion from the disturbing thought. Dwell on this for 30–40 seconds, then slowly allow real-world demands back into your mind. If the anxiety returns, stop it in the same manner, and continue until the cycle of anxiety or guilt is broken.

Relaxation and Meditation

One of the major complaints of dual-career couples is extreme tiredness. For this reason training in relaxation techniques is useful.

Transcendental meditation (TM) is a useful technique to help rid the body of tension.[18] Meditation involves concentrating on a mantra, or single word, for approximately 20 minutes twice a day. This restricts one's mental and physical state and creates a tranquil state of mind and body, which can eliminate stress, improve physical and mental health and increase efficiency. Forty minutes a day may seem excessive to people with busy schedules, especially those who have young children and may find it difficult to find any time at all for themselves. Nevertheless the benefits of meditation should be borne in mind when working out priorities and time management programmes. A more tranquil parent who is unavailable for 20 minutes twice a day may have more to offer children than a harassed one who is constantly available. Meditation may also enable you to accomplish more in a shorter time because of the improved performance it brings about.

Other useful relaxation techniques are progressive muscle relaxation and visualization. There are many commercially available tapes which can be used to aid relaxation. Alternatively you may relax by using the following simple procedure. Tense and then relax the muscles of each part of the body in turn: the left leg, right leg, left arm, right arm, lower half of the body, chest, shoulders, neck and face. Then when the body is completely relaxed visualize a pleasant scene, real or imaginary. Take your time doing this exercise and it will help to reduce tension and renew energy.

Conclusion

The effectiveness of developing work–family management skills will be constrained by the degree to which wider organizations are changing in response to the new workforce. The aim of training programmes should be to facilitate change at work and at home rather than enabling individuals to cope with work and family demands in traditional systems. A primary objective of training is, therefore, to raise awareness of dual-career issues throughout the organization, complementing and not substituting for, policy changes which recognize employees' family demands and responsibilities. Some of these changes are discussed in the next chapter.

8 Changing Organizations

Perhaps one of the major benefits of the emergence and growth of the dual-career family is the demand for a more balanced lifestyle. Men and women alike want room in their lives for both work and family. No longer are large numbers of professionals and executives happy to sell their soul to the company, although many still do so reluctantly, and at considerable personal cost. As one male sales manager we interviewed suggested:

> I don't think my firm recognize that I have family commitments – I am not sure that they even recognize that I'm human! I'm a robot to them, a machine which owes its loyalty and its time to the company.

Major changes have occurred within the family. Many women and men both have careers and ambitions, but neither have the support of a full-time helpmate. If both partners conform to the workaholic lifestyle demanded by numerous companies, there will be many dissatisfied families, as well as a highly stressed and ultimately inefficient workforce. In the previous chapter we explored strategies you can use to reduce and cope with the stress of the dual-career lifestyle, and the training implications. These techniques are unlikely to be totally effective if the workplace is unresponsive to your family needs. Clearly, organizations must play an important role in responding to the needs and expectations of today's workforce. It has to be recognized that the policies of yesterday, which were suitable for families in which there was a rigid division of labour, are no longer appropriate.

Many successful companies are already acknowledging the need for change, and are leading the way by relinquishing traditional practices in favour of policies and practices which accommodate the needs of families. In this chapter we discuss the need to move beyond changes in formal policies to achieve changes in fundamental workplace cultures, without which family-friendly policies will have limited impact.

Limitations of Family-friendly Policies and Practices

We have seen that 'family friendly' policies can be effective in meeting some employee needs[1] and to be of benefit to organizations in terms of reduced absenteeism, enhanced recruitment and retention, and organizational attachment.[2] There are, however, several limitations to the family-friendly provisions currently available, which reduce their potential wider impact. These include:

▌ *Limited access.* These initiatives have mostly been introduced into larger organizations. As such, the majority of employees, especially those with the greatest needs, will be unaffected by these developments.[3]

▌ *Most initiatives are targeted at women and particularly mothers of young children.*[4] This overlooks the diversity in family needs. Consequently, policies tend to enable women to continue in employment while also carrying out their traditional caring roles. The take-up of benefits by men is low, not least because many workplace cultures, and particularly line-managers, still implicitly (if not explicitly) define 'the family' as a concern of women workers.

| *Family-friendly initiatives do not challenge traditional organizational values.* They tend to be regarded as benefits for marginalized workers rather than being integrated into mainstream thinking. The ideal of 'standard' full time, inflexible work,[5] the notion that time in the workplace symbolizes commitment,[6] and the prevailing model of hierarchical and unbroken careers, all remain largely untouched.

| *Formal work–family policies do not necessarily alter informal practices.* Informal practice appears to be heavily influenced by the gender composition of the workforce and can be a powerful factor for, or barrier to, flexibility.[7] Inadequate communication of policies or lack of training for managers in their implementation can be barriers to to the impact of formal policies.

| *Organizations alone cannot support the social change needed for the reconciliation of work and family.* Social as well as organizational policy needs to reflect changing realities. In countries which accept the dual-earner family as the norm, the quality of childcare is monitored by government ensuring that parents have time for family care.[8] However, family policy in the UK, like in the US, tends to be based on the assumption that male breadwinner families remain the norm,[9] with a subsequent lack of support for work and family. Employers may take steps to assist their own employees, but cannot provide overall entitlements or an infrastructure of quality care for all dependants. For this reason the group Employers, for Childcare, a group of leading-edge employers, are campaigning for the government to be more involved in the development of an infrastructure of childcare for all.

Beyond 'Family-friendly' Policies

It is increasingly being argued that for wider change to occur to meet the needs of today's workforce and contemporary organizations, there is a need to move away from a benefits approach of 'family-friendly' policies towards in-built change within organizations.[10] There needs to be a synergy between the needs of various groups,[11] or mutual flexibility at work.[12] Flexibility in this context means taking into account the needs of *all* stakeholders, not just employers' short-term needs. This approach recognizes the diverse needs and identities of workers, including their family roles, emphasises the rights and responsibilities of both employers and employees, moves away from beliefs that there is one best way to accomplish business goals, and seeks ways of meeting mutual goals. This approach implicitly recognizes that many long-standing assumptions about work and family can be modified to meet current needs. This process of questioning traditional assumptions is necessary for meeting the needs of dual-earner couples and their employers.

An Agenda for Change

There now needs to be a forum for discussion where all stakeholders can develop a shared vision of the sort of organizations, families and society we wish to develop and support. The need is particularly great now, not least because of the effects that the pace of economic change is having on the way companies manage their human resources. They offer scope to become more people-friendly, or more alienating.

The necessary changes will involve a number of steps:

▌ *Integrating of work–family issues into core thinking and strategic planning in organizations.* Organizations need to be proactive. They need to anticipate the changing needs of the workforce in strategic planning. That is, they must recognize that the ways in which organizations have operated in the past are not necessarily appropriate to today's workplace.

More diversity in decision making. It is not necessarily the most rational decision outcomes which are acted upon in organizations, but often the decision outcome favoured by the most powerful individual or groups of individuals.[13] Often these are men with non-career wives or women without family commitments. For example, in a recent study of over 1300 US male executives over 50 per cent of those who were married had non-working wives. Although these men reported some interference of work with family, they reported little interference from family with work.[14] It is unlikely that this group will have an understanding of the work–family issues confronting more typical members of the workforce, nor the stress that standard ways of working can create for dual-earner couples. More diversity in decision-making may help to focus organizations on issues relating to the achievement of balance in people's lives.

A rethinking of notions of time. The assignment of value to _time_ varies across time and place. Currently, men's time is valued more than women's, and time in the marketplace more than time with family. These values reflect cultural ideologies, values and beliefs.[15] This influences the sexual division of labour in the home, and the assumed rights of employers to demand excess time which would otherwise be given to family, community or leisure activities. A critical evaluation of the ways in which values are assigned to time will be a necessary precursor to changes to benefit all stakeholders. Within the workplace the definition of time as symbolic of productivity, commitment and value, belittles the contribution of those who work shorter or more flexible hours and disguises the fact that long hours at the workplace reflect inefficiency.[16] Different ways of thinking about time in the workplace might include a focus on quality of outcome rather than quantity of time spent on activities.

Developing flexibility and autonomy. It is only in the context of new ways of thinking about time that genuine flexibility can be achieved and those working non-'standard' hours can be valued as highly as those working in traditional ways. To achieve this, there needs to be openness about the expectations of particular jobs and the demands they make on incumbents' personal lives as a means of clarifying boundaries and an acknowledgement that people can be highly committed contributors to both work and family life.

Redefining careers. A separation of career stage from age and a valuing of a wider range of career patterns is needed. Organizations need people who can do different types of work at different times and be flexible in a way which is currently not encouraged by the traditional career ladder. If careers, as well as time and commitment, can be redefined, this will have important effects. For example, a temporary lower time investment at work to enable individuals to meet family needs, would reduce only the tasks which people are allocated at a particular stage and not undermine what they can achieve in the future. This will be easier to achieve in flatter, less hierarchical organizations.[17]

New approaches to management. Traditional management theory and supervisor behaviour presume a work–family split and assume that a concern for family will interfere with organizational needs. Traditionally supervisors have tended to think in terms of forcing workers to prioritize career or family rather than considering ways of helping them to integrate and manage both. Managing a flexible workforce requires trust, support rather than control, and collaboration rather than confrontation, in finding mutually acceptable ways of achieving goals. Supervisors must still expect workers to meet standards of performance and achieve strategic goals. However, this need not involve denying people autonomy to manage work and family demands.

Reconstructing notions of equality. It is important to clarify the forms of equality we wish to pursue. Definitions of equal opportunities in terms of treating people the same has led to policies that enable women to act like men in the workplace, rather than questioning overall the appropriateness of current work practices for both sexes. There is now a growing awareness of the need to not treat all people the same, but to recognize differences and seek equity and fairness in the workplace. Collaboration and mutual problem solving will enable employees to make an optimum contribution in the workplace.

This will include questioning why women, not men, are deemed responsible for family matters, even though fathers of young children also suffer stress at work through lack of an employer's flexibility.[18] This attitude reinforces the continuing inequality in the sexual division of domestic labour,[19] which in turn is reinforced by gendered expectations in the workplace, so family roles will also have to be considered in wider debates. In a wider context, the growing gap between those in and out of work should also be considered. The long hours of work expected in many organizations, especially at higher levels, together with the poor conditions attached to part-time work and rising unemployment, create a situation in which some people are working too many hours and are unable to make time for family, while others have too little work and can offer little security for their families.

▌*Redefining success.* Success is another dynamic and changing concept and it is useful to reflect on its meaning in the context of current changes and tensions. As Charles Handy points out,[20] successes such as the invention of the motor car or of new manufacturing technology were made without thought to the long-term consequences such as pollution or a redundant workforce. It is important to consider the possible long-term impact of the ways in which we currently define success. Current emphasis tends to be on profits and responsibilities to shareholders, and these are assumed to be independent of other needs.

In a recent Institute of Management national survey of management training and development needs,[21] an increasing awareness of corporate social responsibility, with organizations considering the impact of their operations on a wider range of stakeholders, was identified as an emerging issue. Similarly a report on ways of achieving sustainable business growth in the face of substantial global competition argues that tomorrow's company will have to adopt an inclusive approach to the definition of success, considering all stakeholders.[22]

▌*Public policy support and partnership with industry.* Public policy-makers also need to recognize the changes in family structures and to adapt to meet the needs of these families, recognizing that the single breadwinner family is no longer the norm.

An infrastructure of quality childcare, eldercare and other care is a basic need of all working families. Government has an important role to play here, in partnership with local government and employers if appropriate, to ensure that local needs are met. Social policy-makers also need to consider the value of statutory entitlement to appropriate paid leave for family care. Lack of provision for family leave is based on the assumption that one family member (usually the woman) is either not employed or that their income in not necessary for family upkeep. There is evidence[23] that the costs of providing leave can be balanced by benefits for employers and for the economy as a whole. Apart from the more obvious advantages of greater sex equality, reduced stress and absenteeism, there is some evidence that parental leave encourages androgynous behaviour[24] and this blurring of traditional male/female roles is increasingly recognized as a characteristic of good.[25]

Legislation can also play an important role in the reconciliation process by ensuring equal employment protection for those who work what are currently constructed as atypical hours, to enable them to achieve a balance between work and family. This would discourage organizations from regarding part of the workforce as peripheral and expendable but may be opposed on the grounds of limiting competitiveness. However, the law already defines what are legitimate forms of competitiveness. For example, competitiveness on the grounds of child labour is not acceptable in the Western world, and certain levels of health and safety are also prescribed. Jeremy Lewis[26] argues that if we accept the principle of equality of opportunities it should also be acceptable to define the boundaries of competitiveness, with regard to the type of society we wish to live in. He argues that the law can play a part in the reconciliation of work and family. In the UK, for example, discrimination law has been used to challenge individual employers' decisions not to offer certain forms of flexible work. Nevertheless, some employers find this an unwelcome intrusion and are reluctant to change. This is why both family and corporate needs will be best met via collaboration and problem-solving by all social partners.

Membership of the EC and particularly the Social Chapter may facilitate dialogue between employers and employees and their representatives. Ultimately this may lead to improvements in state policies on maternity, paternity, parental and family leave, childcare and eldercare, and equal opportunities. Meanwhile, employers who understand the needs of the contemporary workforce and the implications for the success of organizations, will lead the way.

Barclays Technology Services: confronting the long hours culture

In 1995 the voluntary organization Parents at Work ran a high-profile national campaign on the long hours culture, designed to raise awareness of the issue and of possible ways of resolving it. Campaign packs sent to employers and individuals, and media coverage all drew attention to the impact of long hours on families and employees as well as negative effects on productivity. The campaign contributed to an awareness that parents and others often work longer than is really necessary just in order to be seen continuously in the workplace. The campaign included a national Go Home on Time Day.

Barclays Technology Services (BTS), a division of the Barclays Group, took this campaign seriously and continues to confront the issue. Barclays has a long-established equal opportunities programme which includes, for example, opportunities for job sharing, career breaks, responsibility breaks and part-time work. However, as we have seen in previous chapters workplace culture can limit the effectiveness of formal policies. BTS, which is male-dominated, is now taking this a step further by confronting the culture of long hours which makes it difficult to balance work and home.

The BTS campaign directly challenges the belief that it is necessary to work long hours to show commitment, and communicates the benefits of achieving a balance between work and non-work time. They have held a number of Go Home on Time

Days, all supported by posters, handouts and articles in their internal newsletter, which aim to raise awareness of the benefits of balancing work and non-work time and to promote examples of good practice. Employees are urged to work smarter, not harder, and are given tips about how to achieve this. For example they are encouraged to think of the amount of time spent on travel or in meetings and to consider alternatives such as phoning, video conferencing, or at least combining visits to cut down on travel time. Other tips include the importance of considering whether meetings are really necessary, and if they are deemed essential, to ensure that meetings are well-prepared with clear aims. The need to prioritize, delegate and empower others to act is also emphasized. These and other strategies aim to save time and increase effectiveness so that work can be accomplished within a normal working day.

To ensure that the message is taken on board by managers, BTS is also running a series of management training programmes to encourage more effective balance of work/non-work time and more effective use of time at work.

References

Chapter 1

1 Lewis, S., D. Israeli and H. Hootsmans (eds) (1992) *Dual-earner Families. International Perspectives*, London, Sage Publications.
2 Brannen, J., P. Meszaros, H. Moss and G. Poland (1994) *Employment and Family Life. A Review of Research in the UK (1980–1994)*, London, Department of Employment.
3 Newell, S. (1993) 'The superwoman syndrome: gender differences in attitudes towards equal opportunities at work and towards domestic responsibilities at home' *Work, Employment and Society*, vol 7 pp 275–89.
4 Wilkinson, H. (1994) *No Turning Back. Generations and the Genderquake*, London, Demos.
5 Schor, J. (1991) *The Overworked American*, New York, Basic Books.
6 Bruce, W. and C. Reed (1994) 'Preparing supervisors for the future workforce: the dual income couple and the work family dichotomy' *Public Administration Review*, vol 54 pp 36–43.
7 Baruch, G. and R. Barnett (1983) *Lifeprints: New Patterns of Love and Work for Today's Women*, New York, McGraw Hill.
8 Neal, M., N. Chapman, B. Ingersoll-Dayton and A. Amlen (1993) *Balancing Work and Caregiving for Children, Adults and Elders*, London, Sage Publications.

9   Ganster, D.C. and J. Schaubroeck (1991) 'Work stress and employee health' *Journal of Management*, vol 17 pp 235–71.

10 Lewis, S. and C.L. Cooper (1987) 'Stress in two earner couples and stage in the life cycle' *Journal of Occupational Psychology*, vol 60 pp 289–303.

11 Lewis, S. and C.L. Cooper (1988) 'The transition to parenthood in two earner couples' *Psychological Medicine*, vol 18 pp 477–86.

12 Quick, J.C., D.J. Nelson and J.D. Quick (1990) *Stress and Challenge at the Top. The Paradox of the Healthy Executive*, John Wiley.

13 Thomas, L.T. and D.C. Ganster (1995) 'Impact of family supportive work variables on work family conflict and strain: A control perspective' *Journal of Applied Psychology*, vol 80 pp 6–15.

14 Institute of Personnel and Development (1996) 'Managing diversity' an IPD position paper.

15 Hammond, V. and V. Holton (1991) *A Balanced Workforce. Achieving Cultural Change for Women: A Comparative Study*, Ashridge Management Research Group.

16 Fletcher, J. and R. Rapoport (1996) 'Work family issues as a catalyst for organizational change' in S. Lewis and J. Lewis (eds) *The Work-Family Challenge. Rethinking Employment*, London, Sage Publications.

Chapter 2

1   Lewis, S. (1997) 'Family friendly policies a route to changing organizational change or playing around at the margins' *Gender, Work and Organization*, vol 4 pp 13–23.

2   Lewis, S. and C.L. Cooper (1996) 'Balancing the work-home interface: a European perspective' *Human Resource Management Review*, vol 5 pp 289–308.

3 Thomas, L.T. and D.C. Ganster (1995) 'Impact of family supportive work variables on work family conflict and strain: a control perspective' *Journal of Applied Psychology*, vol 80 pp 6–15.
4 Lewis, S. and C.L. Cooper (1987) 'Stress in two earner couples and stage in the life cycle' *Journal of Occupational Psychology*, vol 60 pp 289–303.
5 Lewis, S and K. Taylor (1996) 'Evaluating the impact of family friendly employment policies: a case study' in S. Lewis and J. Lewis (eds) *The Work–Family Challenge. Rethinking Employment*, London, Sage Publications.
6 Burke, R.J., T. Weir and R.E. Dulvors (1979) 'Type A behaviour of administrators and wives' reports of marital satisfaction' *Journal of Applied Psychology*, vol 59 pp 9–14.
7 Zedeck, S. (1992) 'Exploring the domain of work and family concerns', in S. Zedeck (ed.) *Work, Family and Organizations*, San Francisco, Jossey-Bass.
8 Meijman, A. (1996) 'When does work end?' Paper presented at international conference on *Work and Family in Europe, East and West*, University of Groningen, the Netherlands.
9 Kingston, P.W. and S.L. Nock (1985) 'Consequences of the family work day' *Journal of Marriage and the Family*, vol 47 pp 620–29.
10 Hall, D.T. (1971) 'A model of coping with role conflict: the role behaviour of college educated women' *Administrative Science Quarterly*, 1, 7, pp 471–86.

Chapter 3

1 Weitzman, C. (1992) 'A theoretical framework for the process of planning to combine career and family roles' *Applied and Preventative Psychology*, vol 3 pp 15–22.
2 Hochschild, A. (1989) *Second Shift: Working Parents and the Revolution in the Home*, New York, Viking Penguin.

3   Mederer, H.J. (1993) 'Division of labor in two-earner homes: task accomplishment versus household management as critical variables in perceptions about family work' *Journal of Marriage and the Family*, vol 55 pp 133–45.

4   Brannen, J. and P. Moss (1992) 'British households after maternity leave' in S. Lewis, D. Izraeli and H. Hootsmans (eds) *Dual-earner Families. International Perspectives*, London, Sage Publications.

5   Newell, S. (1993) 'The superwoman syndrome: gender differences in attitudes towards equal opportunities at work and towards domestic responsibilities at home' *Work, Employment and Society*, vol 7 pp 275–89.

6   Hertz, R. (1992) 'Financial affairs. Money and authority in dual earner marriage' in Lewis, Izraeli and Hootsmans, *Dual Earner Families*.

7   Brannen, J. and P. Moss (1987) 'Dual earner households: women's financial contributions after the birth of the first child' in J. Brannen and G. Wilson (eds) *Give and Take in Families. Studies in Resource Distribution*, London, Unwin Hyman.

8   Potuchek, J.L. (1992) 'Employed wives orientation to breadwinning: a gender theory analysis' *Journal of Marriage and the Family*, vol 55 pp 133–45.

9   Bielby, W.T. and D.D. Bielby (1992) 'I will follow him: family ties, gender role beliefs and reluctance to relocate for a better job' *American Journal of Sociology*, vol 97 pp 1241–67.

10 Lewis, S. and C.L. Cooper (1987) 'Stress in two earner couples and stage in the life cycle' *Journal of Occupational Psychology*, vol 60 pp 289–303; and W.W. Philliber and D.V. Hiller (1983) 'Changes in marriage and wife's career as a result of the relative occupational attainment on wife's achievement' *Journal of Marriage and the Family*, vol 52 pp 323–9.

11 Vannoy, D. and W.W. Philliber (1992) 'Wife's employ-
    ment and quality of marriage' *Journal of Marriage and the
    Family*, vol 54 pp 387–98.
12 Cooper, C.L. (1996) 'Corporate relocation polices' in S.
    Lewis and J. Lewis (eds) *The Work–Family Challenge.
    Rethinking Employment*, London, Sage Publications.
13 Davidson, M. and C.L. Cooper (1983) *Stress and the
    Woman Manager*, Oxford, Martin Robertson.

Chapter 4

1 Lewis, S. and C.L. Cooper (1988) 'The transition to
   parenthood in two earner couples' *Psychological Medicine*
   vol 18 pp 477–86.
2 Brannen, J. and P. Moss (1991) *Managing Mothers. Dual
   Earner Households After Maternity Leave*, London, Unwin
   Hyman.
3 Elliott, S.A., J.P. Watson and D.I. Brough (1985)
   'Transition to parenthood in British couples' *Journal of
   Reproductive and Infant Psychology* vol 22 pp 295–308.
4 Lewis, S., C. Kagan and P. Heaton (1996) 'Dual earner
   parents with disabled children: pressures, needs and
   supports' Manchester, Manchester Metropolitan University, IOD group occasional paper.
5 The voluntary organization, Parent at Work, offers
   annual prizes for the most family-friendly organizations
   in the private and public sectors. PAW has both individual and corporate memberships, offers support to
   working parents and promotes good organizational
   practice.
6 Burnell, A and J. Goodchild (1996) *Developing Work and
   Family Services*, London, Exploring Parenthood.

Chapter 5

1 Sekaran, U. (1985) 'The paths to mental health: an exploratory study of husbands and wives in dual career families' _Journal of Occupational Psychology_, vol 58 no 2 pp 129–38.
2 Greenhaus, J.H. and R.E. Kopemlman (1981) 'Conflict between work and non-work roles. Implications for the career planning process' _Human Resource Planning_, vol 4 pp 1–10.
3 Lewis, S. (1991) 'Motherhood and/or employment: the impact of social and organizational values' in A. Phoenix, A. Woollett, and E. Lloyd (eds) _Motherhood. Meanings, Practices and Ideologies_, London, Sage Publications.
4 Bowlby, J. (1953) _Childcare and the Growth of Love_, Harmondsworth, Penguin.
5 Hoffman, L.W. (1989) 'Effects of maternal employment in the two parent family' _American Psychologist_, vol 44 pp 283–92.
6 Sandburg, D.F., A.A. Ehrhardt, C.A. Mellins, S.E. Ince and H.F.L. Meyer-Bahjburg (1987) 'The influence of individual and family characteristics on career aspirations of girls during childhood and adolescence' _Sex Roles_, vol 16 pp 649–67.
7 Gilbert, L.A. and L.S. Dancer (1992) 'Dual earner families in the United States and adolescent development' in S. Lewis, D.N. Izraeli and H. Hootsmans (eds) _Dual Earner Families. International Perspectives_, London, Sage Publications.
8 Gold, D. and D. Andres (1978) 'Comparisons of adolescent children with employed or non employed mothers' _Merrill Palmer Quarterly_ vol 24 no 4 pp 243–54.
9 Solberg, A. (1990) 'Negotiating childhood: changing constructions of age for Norwegian children' in A. James and A. Prout (eds) _Constructing and Reconstructing Childhood_, London, Falmer Press.

10 Lewis, S., J. Sixsmith and C. Kagan (1996) 'Children in dual career families' in M. Moore, J. Sixsmith and K. Knowles (eds) *Children's Reflections on Family Life*, London, Falmer.

11 op. cit.; and R. Abramaritch and L. Johnson (1992) 'Children's perceptions of parental work' *Canadian Journal of Behavioural Science*, vol 24 pp 319–32.

12 Lewis, S. and C.L. Cooper (1987) 'Stress in two earner couples and stage in the life cycle' *Journal of Occupational Psychology*, vol 60 pp 289–303.

13 Brayfield, A. (1995) 'Juggling jobs and kids: the impact of employment schedules on fathers caring for children' *Journal of Marriage and the Family*, vol 57 pp 321–32.

14 Carro, G. (1983) 'Stay home fathers' superkids' *Psychology Today*, vol 17 p 71.

15 Pleck, J.H. (1985) *Working Wives/Working Husbands*, Beverley Hills, California, Sage Publications.

16 Gilbert, L.A. (1985) *Men in Dual Career Families*, LEA.

17 European Commission Network on Childcare (1996) *A Review of Services for Young Children in the European Union*, European Commission Directorate General.

18 Harrell, J.E. and C.A. Ridley (1975) 'Substitute childcare, maternal employment and the quality of mother-child interaction' *Journal of Marriage and the Family*, vol 27 pp 556–63.

19 Lewis, S. with A. Watts and C. Camp (1996) 'Developing and implementing policies. the Midland Bank experience' in S. Lewis and J. Lewis (eds) *The Work–Family Challenge. Rethinking Employment*, London, Sage Publications.

20 Lewis, S., C. Kagan and P. Heaton (1996) 'Dual earner parents with disabled children: pressures, needs and supports', Manchester, Manchester Metropolitan University IOD group occasional paper; and C. Kagan, S. Lewis and P. Heaton (1997) 'The context of work and caring for parents of disabled children' Manchester,

Manchester Metropolitan University IOD group occasional paper.

21 Kagan, Lewis and Heaton (1997/98) Report to be published for the Joseph Rowntree Foundation, _Parents combining working with caring for children with disabilities_ Bryson, Ford and White (1997) _Lone mothers, employment and well-being_, Findings, September 1997, Joseph Rowntree Foundation.

22 Reuben Ford and Jane Millar (1997) _Private lives and public responses: lone parenthood and future policy_, Foundations, July 1997, Joseph Rowntree Foundation, York.

23 Kamerman, S.B. and A.J. Kahn (1987) _The Responsive Workplace. Employers and a Changing Workforce_, New York, Columbia University Press.

24 Laczsco, F. and S. Noden (1992) 'Eldercare and the labour market: combining care and work' in F. Laczsco and C. Victor (eds) _Social Policy and Elderly People_, Aldershot, Avebury.

25 Phillips, J. (1995) _Working Carers_, Aldershot, Avebury.

Chapter 6

1 Lewis, S. and K. Taylor (1996) 'Evaluating the impact of family friendly employment policies: a case study' in S. Lewis and J. Lewis (eds) _The Work–Family Challenge. Rethinking Employment_, London, Sage Publications.

2 Bensahel, J. (1978) 'Why competition may not always be healthy' _International Management_, October, vol 23 p 5.

3 Lee, R.A. (1983) 'Flexitime and conjugal roles' _Journal of Occupational Behaviour_, vol 4 pp 297–315.

4 Kamerman, S.B. and A.J. Khan (1987) _The Responsive Workplace. Employers and a Changing Labor Force_, New York, Columbia University Press.

5 Labour Force Survey, 1996.

6 Teriet, B. (1985) 'Flexible working years' in D. Clutter-buck, *New Patterns of Work*, Aldershot, Gower, pp 98–194.
7 (1994) *Changing Places. A Manager's Guide to Working from Home*, London, New Ways to Work.
8 *Clerical Teleworking. How it affects Family Life*, a report by BT Research Laboratories, BT.
9 Hill, E.J., A.J. Hawkins and B.C. Miller (1997) 'Perceived influences of mobile teleworkers' *Family Relations*, vol 45 no 3 pp 293–301.
10 Walton, P. (1995) *Balanced Lives*, New Ways to Work.
11 Lewis, S., C. Kagan and P. Heaton (1996) 'Dual earner parents with disabled children: pressures, needs and supports' Manchester, Manchester Metropolitan University, IOD group occasional paper.

Chapter 7

1 Pearns and R.S. Kandola (1994) *Managing the Mosaic. Diversity in Action*, London, IPTD.
2 Quick, J.C., D.J. Nelson and J.D. Quick (1990) *Stress and Challenge at the Top. The Paradox of the Healthy Executive*, Wiley.
3 Gonyea, J. and B. Googins (1992) 'Linking the worlds of work and family. Beyond the productivity trap' *Human Resources Management*, vol 31 pp 209–26.
4 Kagan, C., S. Lewis and P. Heaton (1997) 'Developing organisational audits to support parents combining employment with the care of disabled children' Manchester, Manchester Metropolitan University, IOD group occasional paper.
5 Rapoport, R. and R.N. Rapoport (1971) *Dual Career Families*, London, Penguin.
6 Hall, D.T. (1972) 'A model of coping with role conflict: the role behaviours of college educated women' *Administrative Science Quarterly*, vol 1 no 7 pp 471–86.

7 Alpert, D. and A. Culbertson (1987) 'Daily hassles and coping strategies of dual earner and non dual earner women' *Psychology of Women Quarterly*, vol 11 pp 359–66.
8 Harrison, A.O. and J.H. Minor (1978) 'Interrole conflict, coping strategies and satisfaction among black working wives' *Journal of Marriage and the Family*, vol 40 pp 799–805.
9 Gilbert, L.A., C.K. Holohan and L. Manning (1981) 'Coping with conflict between professional and maternal roles' *Family Relations*, pp 319–426.
10 Yogev, S. (1982) 'Are professional women overworked? Objective versus subjective perceptions of role loads' *Journal of Occupational Psychology*, vol 55/3 pp 165–70.
11 King, A., R. Winnett and S. Lovett (1986) 'Enhancing coping behaviours in at risk populations' *Psychological Therapy*, vol 17 pp 57–66.
12 Cooper, C.L., R.D. Cooper and L. Eaker (1988) *Living with Stress*, Harmondsworth, Penguin.
13 Price, V.A. (1982) *The Type A Behaviour Pattern. A Model for Research and Practice*, New York, Academic Press.
14 Burke, R.J., T. Weir and R.E. Dulvors (1979) 'Type A behaviour of administrators and wife's reports of marital satisfaction' *Journal of Applied Psychology*, vol 59 pp 9–14.
15 Kobasa, S.C., S.R. Maddi and S. Kahn (1987) 'Hardiness and health: a prospective study' *Journal of Health and Social Behaviour*, vol 42/1 pp 168–77.
16 Paloma, M.M. (1972) 'Role conflict and the married professional women', in C. Safilios-Rothschild (ed) *Towards a Sociology of Women*, Lexington, Xerox College Publishing.
17 Schafer, R.B. and P.M. Keith (1980) 'Equity and depression among married couples' *Social Psychology Quarterly*, vol 43/4 pp 430–35.
18 Bloomfield, H.H, G.S. Cain, D.T. Jaffe and R.B. Kory (1976) *TM. How Meditation Can Reduce Stress*, London, Allen and Unwin.

Chapter 8

1 Thomas, L.T. and D.C. Ganster (1995) 'Impact of family supportive work variables on work family conflict and strain: a control perspective' *Journal of Applied Psychology*, vol 80 pp 6–15.

2 Grover, S.L. and K.J. Crooker (1995) 'Who appreciates family responsive human resource policies? The impact of family friendly policies on the organizational attachment of parents and non parents' *Personnel Psychology*, vol 48 pp 271–88.

3 Brannen, J., P. Meszaros., H. Moss. and G. Poland (1994) *Employment and Family Life. A Review of Research in the UK (1980–1994)*, London, Department of Employment.

4 Seyler, D.L., P.A. Monroe and J.C. Garand (1995) 'Balancing work and family. the role of employer supported childcare benefits' *Journal of Family Issues*, vol 16 pp 170–93.

5 Raabe, P. (1996) 'Constructing pluralistic work and career arrangements that are family and work friendly', in S. Lewis and J. Lewis (eds) *The Work–Family Challenge. Rethinking Employment* London, Sage Publications.

6 Hewitt, P. (1993) *About Time. The Revolution in Work and Family Life*, London, Rivers Oram Press.

7 Holt, H. and T. Thaulow (1996) 'Formal and informal flexibility in the workplace', in *The Work–Family Challenge*.

8 Madsen, A.L. (1994) 'Danish policies with respect to children and families with children', in B. Arves-Pares (ed.) *Building Family Welfare* Stockholm: The Network of Nordic Focal Points of the International Year of the Family.

9 Pascall, G. (1986) *Social Policy. A Feminist Analysis*, London, Tavistock.

10 Fletcher, J and R. Rapoport (1996) 'Work-family issues as a catalyst for organizational change', in *The Work–Family Challenge*.

11 Bailyn, L. (1993) _Breaking the Mold. Women, Men and Time in the New Corporate World_, New York, Free Press.

12 Gonyea, J. and B. Googins (1996) 'The restructuring of work and family in the United States: a new challenge for American corporations' in _The Work–Family Challenge._

13 Pettigrew, A. (1993) _The Politics of Organizational Decision Making_, London, Tavistock.

14 Judge, T.A., J.W. Boudreau and R.D. Bretz (1994) 'Job and life attitudes of male executives' _Journal of Applied Psychology_, vol 79 pp 767–82.

15 Schor, J. (1991) _The Overworked American_, New York, Basic Books.

16 Lewis S. and K. Taylor (1996) 'Evaluating the impact of family friendly employment policies: a case study' in _The Work–Family Challenge._

17 Bailyn, L. (1992) 'Issues of work and family in different national contexts: how the United States, Britain and Sweden respond' _Human Resource Management_, vol 31 pp 201–8.

18 Lewis, S. and C.L. Cooper (1987) 'Stress in Two Earner Couples and Stage in the Life Cycle' _Journal of Occupational Psychology_, vol 60 pp 289–303.

19 Newell, S. (1993) 'The superwoman syndrome: gender differences in attitudes towards equal opportunities at work and towards domestic responsibilities at home' _Work, Employment and Society_, vol 7 pp 275–89.

20 Handy, C. (1994) _The Empty Raincoat_, London, Hutchinson.

21 Institute of Management (1994) _Management to the Millennium: The Cannon and Taylor Working Party Reports_, Corby, Institute of Management.

22 Royal Society of Arts report (1994) 'Tomorrow's company, the case for an inclusive approach' London, Royal Society of Arts.

23 Holterman, S. (1995) 'The costs and benefits to British employers of measures to promote equality of opportunity' _Gender, Work and Organization_, vol 2 pp 102–12.

24 Haas, L. and P. Hwang (1995) 'Company culture and men's usage of family leaves in Sweden' *Family Relations*, vol 44 pp 28–36.
25 *Management to the Millennium: The Cannon and Taylor Working Party Reports*.
26 Lewis, J. (1996) 'Work-family reconciliation and the law. Intrusion or empowerment?' in *The Work–Family Challenge*.

Index

Page references in italics indicate tables, exercises and examples